THE HAND
UPON
HIS HEAD

Arthur Gregor

THE HAND
UPON
HIS HEAD

Selected Poems 1947 to 2003

THE SHEEP MEADOW PRESS
RIVERDALE-ON-HUDSON, NEW YORK

All inquiries and permission requests should be addressed to:
The Sheep Meadow Press
P. O. Box 1345
Riverdale-on-Hudson, NY 10471

Designed and typeset by The Sheep Meadow Press.
Distributed by The University Press of New England.

Printed on acid-free paper in the United States. This book meets the guidelines for permanence and durability of the Committee on Production Guidelines for Book Longevity of the Council on Library Resources.

Library of Congress Cataloging-in-Publication Data

Gregor, Arthur, 1923-
  The hand upon his head : selected poems, 1947-2003 / Arthur Gregor.--
1st ed.
     p. cm.
  ISBN 1-931357-16-1 (alk. paper)
  I. Title.
PS3557.R434 A6 2004
811'.54--dc22

                                                        2003020852

We are grateful to the New York State Council on the Arts, a state agency, for their support.

A number of these poems first appeared in *The New Yorker, Poetry, The Southern Review, The Nation*; others in *Sewanee Review, Hudson Review, Kenyon Review, Ploughshares, Paris Review, Quarterly Review of Literature, Accent, Michigan Quarterly Review, Sonora Review, Niagara Magazine, New Letters, World Literature Today, Pembroke Magazine, Hellcoal Annual, St.Andrew's Review, Voices, Yale Poetry Review, Poetry Northwest, Interim, Cumberland Poetry Review, New York Poetry, Pivot, Quarter Moon, Poetry Now, The New Republic, Commentary, Commonweal, Esquire, Harper's Magazine, The New York Times, Pearl* (Denmark); and were collected in: *Octavian Shooting Targets* (1954), *Basic Movements* (1966), *Figure in the Door* (1968), *A Bed by the Sea* (1970), *Selected Poems* (1971), *The Past Now* (1975), *Embodiment and Other Poems* (1982), *Secret Citizen* (1989), *The River Serpent and Other Poems* (1994), and *That Other Side of Things* (2001).

To Chantal Curtis
and in memory of
Susheela Dayal

"There are a thousand ways of missing the bull's eye, only one of hitting it."

"For what we engender from the soul, the offspring of our mind, our heart, and our talents, springs from parts nobler than the corporeal, and more truly our own. In this act of generation we are father and mother at once; these cost us much dearer and, when there is anything good in them, bring us greater honor as well. For the merits of our other children are much more theirs than ours, the share we have in them being very slight; but all the beauty, all the grace, and all the value of these are our own. They therefore represent us and resemble us more vividly."

— Montaigne

"That which helps us to expand beyond body limits (the arts) must be seen to have emanated from the real Self."

— Sri Atmananda

CONTENTS

I   LOSS

Blackout	2
Poem	4
Poem II	6
Ritual	9
Of Caligula, Bach and the Seascape	11
Octavian Shooting Targets	14

II   RETRIEVAL

First Snow, Brooklyn Harbor	18
Basic Movements	23
Spirits, Dancing	25
A Single Flower of the Field	27
Assisi and Environs	28
Rocks Partly Held in Mist	30
A Tree Unlike Others	31
A Sunbather in Late October	32
Runaway Spirit	34
The Likeness	36
The Calm	38
Cypresses (Postscript)	39
Reply to a Friend in New England	40
Shadowplay	42
Exiled	43
Autumn Mood	44
Don Carlos, Saturday Afternoon	45
Awakening Mystery	46
Late Last Night	48
Irreconcilables	49
Enchanted Flowers	51
Wandlung	55

Some Elements of Drama 57

Encounter at Tehuixtla 59

Lament for a Talent 63

The Mist from Tree to Tree 64

Gentle Lamb 65

Today's Troubadours 67

The Unworldliness That He Creates 68

Short Poem 77

Costa do Sol 78

The Poem 79

Unalterables 80

The Statue 81

Sleep Took Me Far 82

Worldliness 83

Rocky Tarn 84

The Ship 85

Two Poems on the Firebird 90

Perspectives 92

History 94

Old Coat 95

India 97

Unnatural Heat, Moosehead Lake 98

Words of the Pilgrim 100

The Tenuous Line 101

The Look Back 103

Les Nuits d'Été 104

Enough 105

Continuity 106

The Hand upon His Head 107

Two Poems on the Same Figure 115

Frail Perfection 117

On Behalf of Orpheus 118

Wind to Human Voice 119

from Fragments and Short Poems 121

Oiseau Triste 123

Wilderness Child 124

The Door 126

A Defiance 128

At a Traffic Intersection 130

Approaching a Bridge in Northern California 133

The Link 135

Cul-de-Sac 136

To Emily 137

Abundance, Now 138

Two-Sided 139

The Rescue 140

The Kiss 141

A Visit 142

The Pine 143

The Stray 145

The Florist 147

The Shaper of Words on His Instruction 149

In Memory of Jean Garrigue 150

The Power of Art 151

Muse 163

In Dark's Cover 164

The Threshold or, My Home in Winter 167

The Poem of Heaven Within 174

On Another Departure 199

Old Offense 200

Spirit's Taunt 201

Dark Converse 202

Signals 203

77th Street Fair 204

Mozartian 205

Mozart in Châtillon 206

from Memory Fragments 208

Two Swans at Ousson 214

Magician 216

Geraniums 224

Father and Son at St. Benoît   226
The River Serpent   228
Gesualdo   231
Like Marble   233
Yellow Wildflowers   234
Chiaroscuro   237
Aria   241
In Himself Absorbed   243
Disarrangement   244
The Poem, Ousson-sur-Loire   245
Six Days in Prague   247
Portrait   250
At the Beginning of the End of Day   253
Three Autumn Moods   255
The Park   256
So Fleet, So Infinite   284

A Note on the Author   288
Also by Arthur Gregor   289
Selected Reviews and Comments   290

I
LOSS

Blackout

When Europe and romanticism
coasted below resounding blackouts
like an airsick sofa, and Petrarch
sat weeping for wisdom's sake
and the unsung death of lemon bushes,
and Florence coughed out in blood
her ornate fountains of illustrious
merchants, I harbored, O My People,
I harbored mediterranean salons
for white fingers and Scarlatti.

Hitler was an expert at entertaining.
All the world said he was madder
than Caligula. Nevertheless he was
quicker than his own industrialists,
well disposed to great Danes,
and at evening from mountains
pointed out his panorama: smoke
and crematoria, the Simple Right
To Live all gone—and then
"Tara tara tara" on his forest horn.

The sensitive, the disillusioned
in America pantomimed a sad pavane:
Justice dead, the Pure all lost;
and scuttling coffins planted tiny islands
for purity to prosper. It was here
that I looked in, scouting on
my lifeboats murdered rubbish,
and it was here I faced
angels on rococo instruments,
saw the grand staircase where

fantastic shepherds rose wet from
a ridiculous sea, memory   memory

1947

Poem

for Hannelore Axmann

So many pigeons in Columbus
Circle in America; go, Tierra,
go! It is past the wars
and the nuns are waiting at
seaports, at the entrance to
the park. The fountains in the
Villa d'Este are the most
beautiful fountains in all

of Italy, was a statement in
a survey on Western Civili-
zation, and on the Piazza della
Signoria, Perseus is slaying
the Medusa to this day. When
I was 12, I said: patria
nostra olim provincia Romana
erat, and landed, riding on

seahorses of gold, on centuries
and Cellini, bumps in front of
the Doge's palace holding hands
with Beatrice. What an inter-
minable link, I thought, with
many orators and many merchants
and Punchinello, Punchinello,
the idiot of the circus, he

whom we have wrong too
much, Lisa's delight when she
was 4, he who sits on
churchsteps bleeding end-
less harps from his

nailed down fingers, O Tierra,
O witches in a reddening
forest, O whoever, whatever

recalls this all; like certain
young men who turn on an
elegant street, who go on
past cathedrals jittery as
swans and princes who have
missed their cue, who have no
other chance, and have no
other chance. So many dead,

so many murdered, Tierra, and
there was the singer in the
valley of oranges, and there
were the snows, the emerald
crowns on fishes in der Arls-
bergergrotte, and there was
the silence, and there were
the madonnas at noon. . .

Poem II

Also according to the
frescoes at San Lorenzo
there was once a fort-
ress; there were three
kings who rode unto

the city on white mules
contemplating; there were
the beggars and the women
selling alpenflowers.

And when we came to
the valleys of the Tatra
where for centuries
the partisans had put up
tents and fires

we were aware of a
strong smell of hay and
the sounds of horses
galloping across the
meadows and all along

the roadside stood the
saints with a bunch of
cornflowers in the folded
arms and the songs and
the calls at nightfall.

The fog was heavy on
the waters when the

exiles came to the
harbor; there was a world

that was gone or for
better or worse was
going; they came with
the memory of mountains,

laurels, disk throwers
in the noon arena; they
had great feeling for
the few non-belligerent
outposts, the naked pillars
unsought by Aeolus;

they welcomed the
harbor, the other home-
less weeping waiting wet
at the pier.

And when I was a boy
we drove through
the forest with
horses and sleigh

and later when I wore
long trousers and the
warriors came toward me
with spears held at an angle

Surely this is no
confession, you have
seen my shield
by now too obstinate

turn murderer at
my bedside—
surely you have known. . .

Also the medallions of
the Medici were arrayed
in magnificent splendor
and the guilds of Florence
were openly grateful
for so benevolent a family

The foxes were steadily
kept on the grounds
and Catherine bore nobly
her crown throughout
the bloody times of France.

And when I see the dead
swarm about the islands
of fruit, the islands of
yellow fruit and there is

silence and an early fall
of oranges, and I recall
my world, the spears
flashing in the sun

and when I see the high
rocks and the white of
the foam of the sea and hear
tall monks and the marvelous
airs of Monteverdi   O world
O homeless   O fortress

Ritual

To Tiberius the aura of the hot basin,
of towels and oils felt like the
fluffy paleness of flamingoes
and it was here he brought
a book of poems and a small revolver
holding Hindu rivers in his eyes
and virgin bodies yielding to the Holy
Cleansing. Shortly after, his devotee,
a young male servant frantic with
love and shame phoned the police
who knew and therefore never came.

Tiberius meanwhile stood naked, con-
centric to four long mirrors and looked
at himself from four angles. He turned right
and what the mirror translated was
idiomatic of his boyhood, village days,
cornflower fields, of friendship, and of
books and white doves fluttering. He turned
left and saw himself as a barefooted god,
a tourist with a golden haired naiveté
of wisdom, among ceramic horses scattered on

the sands of ancient Rome. It was here
that he had forgotten everything, that he
had found Orpheus, the cries of charioteers,
art, in fact, symbolic of sorrow at a perfect
sunset. The looking glass in front revealed him
as most dexterous in "what life has to offer,"
showed him fingering feathers and medieval
instruments, showed his effluent brown eyes,
whereupon he remarked: "These are the tears
of unfortunate birds upholding rosaries

to monsters in their silver seas."
It was the fourth mirror, showing Tiberius
as then he was, that caused him to throw himself
upon the floor wailing that all this had never been
his wish, but that such was his heritage:
the way of Immortals to outrage crime with crime,
and that he was Tiberius H. the fifth,
rich and 28 and life was much too
short, and so he had tried. It was then
that he stepped into his bath, poems and

revolver on the floor. Twisting in the steam
Tiberius realized his servant's fear and
thought of him: drumbeats, a tropical sunset,
the claws of mild jaguars; and again felt him-
self as being one with primitives and drums,
aware of sacrificial rivers rising uproarious
through lotus thickets, gliding fanatically
through him. And then then the shot was heard.
Buddha and the oriental heavens had done
the virgins wrong, the rivers were bottomless,

they had lost so much and wept bitterly.
The young servant frantic with love and shame
drove a dagger through his throat. The fourth
mirror shot, stood impotent as crumpled cello-
phane: the simulated god of adolescence was
mortal after all and bled profusely. Poets
cried for their poems abused on bathroom floors,
and motors, and throngs of passers-by ignorant of
their potency waited as Tiberius, all dressed,
left the last palace step, out for a good time.

Of Caligula, Bach and the Seascape

The sky and
the blue seascape
and the waves in
normal upsurge
shaped as the boats
in Hat-shepsut's time
by no mere coincidence

bearing the Queen's
gold and carpets
down the sometimes
quiet waters where
later Caligula said
to Neptune

I am the God

and scores drowned
complete with armor
and wine jugs

and the roaring of
the waters was deeper
than the idiot's laughter
blacker than cuttlefish
hit by spear

The sky and
the blue debris
in the blue-white foam
and the seascape blue
when it is calm

the waves and a white
convoy,
swan for more
than mere convenience

is what we have
without question

The sky and
the seascape and
the swan out in the sea
not too far, never too close
bearing theory, ideal,
the silver prince of peace

he who will not strip
to suntan beside us
will not ever

as the blue blue
seascape will never
rush sh sh
against our fingers

but who will ever in
the fold of wings of swans
exist as a Bach Chorale exists

bravura
bravura
in us

The sky and
it is blue in the forum

of scattered salvages,
bone, horn, jade monkeys
that sailors kept,
the blue of soothsayers
and a sterile hand

Tiberius at Capri

we know of leopards and
the feasts of German guards

and the waves and
the swan or a white
basilica

a heritage quite complicated
quite without question

The sky and
the blue seascape
and the horn, the searose

the idiot's laughter,
the prince and
the chorale

the blue debris and
the very small clouds

purple when the coasts
where the lotus grows
turn to the sun

Octavian Shooting Targets

The top hat, French poodle, the electric heart
flaring up at minute intervals,
you needn't run and be alarmed at this—
it is all quite harmless now. He was a god
some years ago, a fashionable myth,
once or twice on the best-seller list, and now
we will have him here. Those who have seen
his picture in newsreel or magazine will
recognize Octavian, looking still like a
late renascence of an adolescent's faded
dream. Before he comes his seconds will
appear but will not fire shots into
the garden air; a team of village cowboys
they will be ready when Octavian shoots
to play for him Cole Porter on Austrian
flutes. You are amazed, you wonder why?
You thought he had the Bible read to him
in bed; listened to Bohemian madrigals sung
by innocents in Nebraskan stables; had corn-
roses put in his hair by dreamy· devotees,
watching from hedges, sitting in trees.
You did not know of this, his daily fate:
he requests to shoot targets each morning
at eight: Octavian, grey-blond, not old,
not young, artist of considerable fame.

The papers do much for glamor; elaborate
on a violent death: statues of Egyptian
ancient kings were found to exhale poisonous
breath in the halls of a southern water-
villa. A handsome farmhand, trained because
he is sufficiently talented by a well-
known, aging playwright-sportsman, has won
the seaskiing trophy in Peru—the rest

is left to the fierce imagination of not
a starving few. How those who had
made it, Octavian for one, had tasted
bitterly in Nebraskan stormy wheat; what
it was that caused it, had long begun
and why; why others must kill themselves,
driven, desperate, afraid to try (the young
man who had put Octavian up before he
had come to fame was found dead on a
subway track at theatre time); what it is
that must be given to get at such gain
and how it is done; how those who
had helped Octavian on, powerful com-
patriots too weak to want vengeance, had
made of him their Nebraskan hero, their
pioneer; how he had lessened their fear;
and now you ask: why is Octavian here?

London took him in but he was bored, Taos,
Portofino and the like where counts and
millionaires have art students to lunch
he touched on briefly; Athens, Florence and
the Villa Borghese he ignored; pursued the
darker shadings of his restless soul to
harbors and a Nepal caravan; came across
a circus, hunting kangaroos, met the aerial
dancer, thought well of a Gypsy chieftain's
wife: believed for days he had found
some life. Interested in the doings of
foreign hordes occupying a foreign country,
in principle anti-hordes but frankly given to
their brutal charm, he gained permit to
a palace built by an American for the benefit
of art, a sort of 20th-century monastery where
only approved artistic expatriates practice

daily rites. And there, catching himself
one night on a secret expedition to an
Arab sacred ritual of 30 chosen sons, he
laughed out, roared a whole night, a clown
among clowns, and was seen publicly once more
before he withdrew, before he was done,
throwing away his flowers riding in a gilded
hearse through the boulevards of busy Oran.

You will find others here. Those who sit
in attic rooms dressed as movie queens
waiting to be interviewed. Audiences with
kings, extraordinary swims, prize winning
models at a Florida review, spin around
the backwalls of needy, furnished minds,
a world where priests sweep dust in corners:
crash as symbols, our clues, out of their
horror–night. Clutching newsreports
to iron window-bars, they sometimes tell
of recollections, quick visions breaking
through their screams: figures at a bath,
David in the square, girl at her clavier.
These are chanced on, a hand to the castout
like artworks found intact in a defeated
town; to one in his night a slender
youth appears, dark and tearful
as if it were childhood burned by sun.
Another minute and we will have Octavian,
brought by attendants to the practice room.
Before he comes his seconds will appear,
but will not fire shots into the garden
air; a team of village cowboys, they will
be ready when Octavian shoots to play
for him Cole Porter on Austrian flutes.

1951

II
RETRIEVAL

First Snow, Brooklyn Harbor

1.

Driven by a music of which their every move
in a mood of love, the loftier side of them
in dreams, are parts; unconsciously out for a sign
that is a gesture of the song they do not hear:
who among those who stopped along the promenade
facing the waterfront could have regarded
the first flake of the first snow this season
as nothing but the substance that each is?

Unless someone had ventured out, had left
the customary ways of recognizing form
and light and shade; unless someone endowed
with a rare inner quality had looked
and found the single substance holding these
flowing from his eyes and breaking from
the heart where it lies and not unlike
calm waters beneath mountains frozen waits
beneath all icy grounds where light like
sound in the unsaid aspect in each song
glistens beyond sight;

                          unless someone had pierced
the surfaces and stood entirely immersed
within the substance of all forms, within
the very center of all thoughts and shapes
that like the very breath of time rise from
the one sure thing toward which all strive;
unless someone in such state had given
existence to the first flake falling and from
beyond the range of sight proclaimed the whiteness
that streaked across the eye in streams

and in a time too imminent to calculate
dissolved, absolved the heaviness of the world:

who among the solitary men looking out
beyond the river and the ocean piers
into a changed and changing distance, could
have known that these are closely linked:
the forms across the waterway, the lights
barely discernible that alternate, the snow
that falls, the physical significance of snow,
the revival in the hearts of solitary men
of dreams?

How could they have known that these
are more than linked, are one with that
which glistens in and between the flakes,
are the same as what the fall of snow implies?

And what it evokes in them, how could they know
it is the same as what they—solitary men,
distances apart, gazing beyond the river,
ocean–landing where they stand—in this
first snow are looking toward, are looking at?

2.

The thing itself that lives, the dominance
of that which is so close to all it is
the heart of all; in which the first sign
originates and descends into sight as snow,
whose nature is unfathomable although
in this and every scene implied by some
incomprehensible means like a music
that cannot be heard: O what they do not know
is that the distances expand within them:
what they are looking toward is where they are.

They do not know departure is the pain they carry;
that circumstance has forced on them a burden
the removal of which is the change they seek
in dreams of a journey and the joy they sense
of what it must be like the instant of arrival.
In a fall of snow, the first of the season,
they stand and dream and watch the footprints
disappear in the will of heaven; absorb the sounds
of water-objects drown in a deeper music,
and shiver as light breaks in their hearts
and something vastly woeful hangs at their eyes.

For, if these men are in no way exceptional,
if they are not endowed with a sacred privilege
to look and find the answer contained in the question,
fire in the ultimate regions of cold, arrival
in the act of departing, the indivisible total
in each divided vanishing footfall
as each flake contains all of the snow.
If it is not for them to set forth
provoking customary habits with
a selfless motive for daring and a song
to rely on from loss to finding, they cannot know this,
though they do surely sense how enormous are
the heights that exist within the pattern of Being:

Beyond their conditioned manner of reaching, near them,
with no more than a turn of their shoulder,
they can glimpse the regions of high-minded men:
the heart which is wisdom, the pleasure, the welcome,
the compassionate quality in music.
The burden circumstance has forced on them
is a condition abolished by a shift within them,
as the heaviness of the world is abolished by

a sudden decision which is the first snow
of the season.

★   ★   ★

               And if they cannot know themselves
possessors of the single substance
of which all of the harbor before them,
and the forms that make up the harbor
and the transformation of everything in
and around them which they attribute to snow,
are made of;
            and if they cannot assume the stand
that that which is in them, into which
each flake dissolves and all perceptions flow,
is changeless, and they the beholder of changes;—

they do, just the same, sense with longing
something of permanence, knowing, as they do,
only the changes; and for a moment absorbed
in a depth that is the quiet of the whiteness
descending, question:

                   what are they caught in?
Where does it come from, the dream, the thoughts
of which they are conscious? Has the snow
brought back the ways they knew as children,
dreams that have caused them embarrassment in gesture,
quick glances?

              And if they cannot recognize
themselves in the radiance of unreal faces
like spirits in a net of snow; and if
what they know is not the supreme conquest
by achievement but the mystery like a sob
within them, they do, just the same, sense it:
the nearness that is far:

ranges of oceans,
distance and music in the sounds of water-objects;
and grieve for the breath of an angel they feel
in the footfall they cling to for an all-engrossing,
all-encompassing vastly beautiful moment
before the outlines that attest to the fact
that a human has been there, turn into snow.

1960

Basic Movements

1.

He moves out of the dark
unto an empty place
a steersman if you like
at the helm in a fog
and what his mind contains
is more likely than not
at odds with rules of the night
and with a ship's log.

He steps with caution
as though a dancer on
an empty stage in sleep
moving in slow motion
his vision not heeded
ignored by the night
a heavy air settled on
city streets and ocean.

2.

He has moved out of the dark
has stepped forth
has lifted up one arm
the other held stretched out

He has opened his mouth
and not a sound
not a ripple
not a whishing in the air

audible, noticeable, anywhere. . .

3.

Therefore must love abound
love arrived at when
good attempts have failed,
brave steerings toward
important ends
have been inadequate.
How shall love be traced?
overhung by haze
nothing as its base. . .

Spirits, Dancing

Having put yourself on the way,
it is inevitable that you
should reach here. If in
your thoughts you've had
the notion of reward
as you fought to come this far,
banish them. And,
as penalty for entering,
shed the attitudes of worldly men
regarding us and this
celestial sphere where now
your spirit begs to enter.

From the extremity
to which you've come, you see
us sway as in a dance.
It is no sign that we
are happy. To be happy
is being a step removed
from happiness. Which we
never are. Nor are we sad.
Sorrow is man in the world,
and we, the total expression
and awareness of his state,
are sorrowful.

What seems to you,
who were taught to feel
we must fulfill
where the world has failed,
must turn to good the bad,
must invoke permanence
for material whose law

and will it is to die—
what seems to you, driven here
by urgency, a dance
is nothing but the pain in the world
which we like a mirror contain.

To sway is to depart
as branches from a stem,
as shadows from foliage
thick and dark—
and to depart is what is pain.
What you must know before
you enter this domain
and learn the ways of which
we shall not speak is this
first truth of what you are:
a sorrow, a sorrow
begging for home. Or you
would not have come this far.

A Single Flower of the Field

A single flower of the field—
one in a great multitude—
not singled out by gatherers
or those who like to speak
of that which is unique,
said to the wind about to tear
it at its root: "Do what you will!

"Your force across this field
stings every vein in me.
Dumbstruck I was when first
you took my pollen and my leaves,
but you have seen yourself in me,
have made me what you are,
and my oblivion has ceased."

Assisi and Environs

The earth more than the relics
and the timely man-made things—
the land's variety richly
developed, valleys and hills,
cedar lanes and olive groves,
a fertile green differing in tone,
the simple country roads and streams—
the scene unified and yielding like a plant
laden with fruit—painters of long ago
have shown this country so—
arches, aqueducts and buildings all
in the same irregular local stone:
the earth more than most other things
suggests now who it was
who once walked over it.

Between the leaves on trees above
the field where a peasant stacks up hay
while his horses graze nearby
and other fully laden carts
are chased by barking dogs,
between the sight of one such scene
and of another, and between
the bells, the many bells,
the sounds of cymbals hang,
of trumpets and of all such instruments
suitable for the processional,
the timid, unobtrusive passing of
the soul in whom the very soil
reflects itself, becomes itself
as the child coming to life in air.

That such have passed here,
have scattered from their sleeve

of coarsest cloth a wind
of jasmine scent, have reigned
as evidence of what is possible
in man, have dispelled the notion
where they dwelled, that man's life
is identical with
the nature of the earth,
have subdued this ignorance
the way an Eastern saint laid low
the deadliest of snakes
by doing no more than lifting up
his hand and walking lightly by
as days go by, and all of time.

To that, to that expression of
the height in man that swept
across these parts as a star
descends across the sky,
to that this land does testify.
Those who seek through living
evidence to understand can catch
between the sounds they hear
the land's perpetual chant
and see beneath the surfaces of trees,
of fields and hills as if beneath a sea
that look of timelessness, of love
in the eyes of those accomplished ones
who walked here once and now still hold
deep in their eyes this land, as of old.

Rocks Partly Held in Mist

The rocks out in this bay
are partly held in mist.
Their ragged top is seen
but at their base a froth–
like substance hangs as if
the element of ice from which
shroud-like vapors rise
clung fiercely to each cliff.

And so with other things
whose upper parts shine in
the light that they have reached,
whose lower half is held
by all the weight and darkness
characteristic of the earth.

The force that hangs around
the base of rocks needs ghosts
and other shapes to fall
like mist across the mind,
to gather strength in bones,
in lack of clarity, in fear.
Slowly the top and upper parts
dissolve in air as air.

A Tree Unlike Others

There is a tree by the lake
bending way out over the water,
straining over the surface,
like a forlorn wanderer
looking down from a bridge
while most of a city sleeps.

Something so aloof, almost lost
about that tree stubbornly
turning away from others,
patiently straining to see
what others along the shore
cannot catch, like those of us who,
unwilling to linger,
go past and see only
the changes that most of us see.

But the tree has left nothing
behind. Straining over the water,
what does he catch
with endurance and calm
but the image of trees?
And what does he see
beneath the sky in the lake
but leaves and birds on a tree's
bent form, and the leaves
and the birds on each arm
that every season
have come and have gone?

A Sunbather in Late October

On the bank of the river
covered by a haze as if
there hung a bird—
its head deep in the sky,
its wings so immense
they are always there—
a young sunbather lay
in the dry grass reclined
as on a bed
waiting to submit
to the power of
the autumn sun whose rays
could scarcely penetrate
the veils of thick white air.

From time to time
behind the haze
a ship appeared
whose bulk looked vague
in the diffusing
manner of the day.
No one could say
if men hung in its masts
dead or alive
intent on
spotting the bird
kept out of sight
by the pervasive glare.

In such anticipation
the young sunbather lay
his legs apart

like a woman, enraptured by
the whir of wings,
waiting for mysterious heat
to sting his bones,
for haze to wipe his body out,
for unexpected magic in the air
like a bird with giant beak
to pick his flesh,
eager to recognize his disembodied self
in the mirror blazing in the air!
Why else was he there?

Runaway Spirit

At night when the streets were still
and most people in the city
had slipped deep into sleep,
a whisper ran down pavements,
air curling like a tornado
whizzing up and down like
a siren or some whistling freak,
a wailing clinging to shut doors,
to windows without life in them.
And this is what it was:
air whining to be earth,
spirit howling for body and face.

And this is what it said,
the freakish thing of air,
the impulse up and down the street
as if it wished to raid
the earth: "Without legs, arms,
without face in the mirror,
without means to attempt
to experience what I am,
without human attributes
what abstract thing am I!
As a tree feels itself most
when a storm tears at its roots,

as lovers who love their love
best when they part, as a traveler
seeing an old town on a hill,
bright roofs and towers like a crown
speeding away from him
feels first what he has lost:
what lives knows itself best

when it is suffering most.
It may be odd of me
to demand again the earth,
who know so well its pain,

but when a city sleeps
and I perceive and feel
what is in people's dreams
no matter what they dream,
I turn into a runaway spirit
willing to give all I can
for life in the flesh again."
And so it wailed and whirred
and all across the city in
the hours between twelve and dawn
this yearning was abroad.

The Likeness

How can you live, how exist
without assurance of
or at least the memory of
someone, something
fantastic, marvelous
always behind you,
a hand, grip on your shoulder,
a presence surrounding you
as a shell surrounds what lives inside?
Song closer to you than flutter to wing!
Words more antique than age!

Without it—call it intimacy,
your intimate connection—
how do you stand vis-à-vis
the multiplicity of things,
a tree, fence, grass, person in your path?
Unless you find in them
that quality no one defines,
how do you love, what do you
whisper, what song
do you share in the dark?

Without it I am as someone
lost from his caravan
a sandstorm whipping him;
someone out to find help on a frozen sea,
man alone on a waste of ice
imagining as the vast and hazy
emptiness absorbs him
a tattered though victorious
humanity coming toward him,
soldiers linking arms,

a populace with banners
singing and beating drums.

Without it
I am cut off.
I await its sound.
I ravage memory
for sight of it, its melody.
I shape with bare
and desperate hands
its likeness in myself.

1966

The Calm

1.

Attempt at all times closeness to
the conflict you are in.
Not so as to dwell upon
dulling details of the cause
but to be aware of this:
that you are always in between
a white-clad calm that
at long intervals comes down
and the steady turmoil at the base:
a sea seething,
a field devastated,
a man weeping, stone and dust
turned human for as long as
being human can be endured.

2.

Closeness to the conflict is
your nearness to its source.
The more fully a singer sings of
the pure anguish of your state,
the deeper the thought in you
that you too are being heard.
The turmoil in the water is often in
the surface that is thin.
When you cry because where you had been
the coast was calm, your small boat
in the sand left upside down,
the white–clad figure moving toward you
spanning sea and sun,
bemoan, bemoan it is no longer so!
The calm that will come again
                    was long ago!

Postscript to "Cypresses"

Cypresses are taller than most trees.
Space shows no mark of strain or tear
due to their stately rise,
due to their heavy fall at death.
To the ancients the cypress was
a proper symbol of the dead
sacred to Pluto of the underworld.
Probably because this tree
ennobles the countryside,
its foliage turns black in time,
or because, popular as
material for musical instruments,
the wood of the cypress has
the properties that art demands.

Reply to a Friend in New England

I have your note.
Sorry to read you're lonely.
You have not found the joy you went for.
I know the bay you're visiting.
There the visual things
suggest the condition you feel,
flap in one's soul
like laundry hung to dry.
The sky is static there,
thin clouds the color of
swans' wings let through
a light that reaches corners
but has not the power
to illuminate.

Water beats against the stones
below the strip where people sit,
the boats out in the bay
look as though they give themselves
to being tossed about,
and not much happens.
The shadow of a bird
(wings spread fully out
the bird seems not to move,
seems painted on the air)
hovers over the reflection in
the water of a boat,
gray spreading over gray.
Shadows in this bay

that seek each other out,
cannot be kept apart,
nor does one blank the other out

escaping thus the separateness
that all decry, the flow
and sway of each with which
each must identify.
Is this then the law
that all must learn to live
who visit where you are
or any other strip of coast:
identity must be retained?
loneliness is part
of being self-contained?

In this bay where you have come,
where the coast is defined
by what you see—
by monotone and static sky—
you like others must confront:
the limited return
of what you want.
All day long the light is faint.
The repeated view of sails,
taken for white flags
implying hope, is bleak.
You have not found another way,
no other way but inward for
the self-assuring joy you seek.

Shadowplay

Dead to the world, I was cast back
to move again among familiar shapes.
The state where I had been
cannot be described. There were
no objects there, but in
full strength and in pure form
the presence that takes speech
and mind away when feelings
are stirred by a person's momentary stay
pale as early evening in the door.

I knew when I was back it was
not nothingness had held me there.
That part in me which bears
no semblance to my body's line
on paper or in falling light
was then about to be received
like a cloth brought to be laid
across arms wide as space,
by a love gentler than air
and voices, voices behind clouds.

Not yet allowed, some forces dark
and fleeting came and drew me back—
from high walks where structures hold
all time and things that pass—
back to shadows that glide across
the shadow of my hands,
back to the movement of clouds,
the light at dark, the noted hush,
the moment of the figure in the door,
back to my repeated effort among
the things where I have walked before.

Exiled

Where will you go? Where now the rooms
once kept ready for you? the old
couple on hand to welcome you,
the garden just as it was when last
you visited, just as it was
as far back as you remember it—
golden the landscape when you stood there
late in the afternoon.

Where is it now, that place where you
belonged so naturally? the formal
growths, the house, the sunset-sights,
the dark turns of corridors—all these
as much alive in you then as they
were real then, summer after summer
in the country not far from town.
Now they are gone. Thoughts of them

stay on like tatters of a sail.
Memory will pale, and you have no
way now to turn and walk into
the interior you knew so well.
Another storm, one final gust,
your tattered thoughts will be as dust.
To keep alive the glow within
of what was once your ground, your home,
you need the plot, the trees, the stone.

Autumn Mood

The smell that flames impart to air
of a fire tended and controlled
in a garden or clearing in
an autumn wood

stirs the recumbent fellow in
the body's inner room
where not a hallway leads,
no easy turn of knob can reach.

Pensive and full
of weeping thoughts he lies,
to a violent strength aroused
when invading smells and sounds proclaim
the burning season dies.

Don Carlos, Saturday Afternoon

Alone! Who does not know the meaning of
alone? Granted, there is a world outside,
houses and streets are wet,
people run in and out of cars.
In the story sung on the air
each character is in the end alone.
A Spanish prince still loves the woman
who has become his father's bride.
A conquering Court attends the saving
of fallen Christians at the stake.
Although one hears a lofty Gloria,
the prince in prison chains cries out,
betrayed, he thinks, by the one he loved
and by the friend in whom he believed.

Does it really help that being alone
is one condition shared by all?
The drama off-stage is no less complex.
Although one may assume that
disparate parts that do not always lock
in place are woven by a common thread,
the burden is not lessened for all that.
Not lessened by bewildered heads
and muffled cries, nor by the fact
that the sky's been agitated all day long,
that men in raincoats stumble across
slippery roofs, and that the very air
is dense with wriggling bacteria
that show up under a powerful glass.

Awakening Mystery

Leaving the place to which you are accustomed,
whose unknown corners you think of
less and less and forget them day
by day; leaving the place whose mystery
is never fully explored
because it has become familiar
and you forget that there is something hidden
behind your door,
something beyond the reach of lights
that you have missed, and do not know.

Leaving the place whose mystery is shrouded
because it has become familiar
and exploring the familiar is usually neglected,
it can happen one day
when you take a train into the country
that you find every road, every field,
every house and stream washed in a clarity,
each enriched by nothing but
its own quality,
a horse grazing here, a bridge over there,
and something that is quick
in the distance, whose shape is lost
but whose shadow you see.

And when you pass a brook
and look down upon the water in absolute stillness,
see the backs of houses, a boat tied to
the bank and you remark: "How still,
how perfectly still it is,
the very black shadow of trees
in the water" and thereafter think
of a woman weeping

because someone had made her understand,
and you are not sure if this was dreamt
or witnessed by you at some time, but know
that her experience at that moment
is something you can comprehend,

and you are moved, so moved
to have somehow been made to possess all this.
It is then, when peace and clarity
take hold of you and you are so at ease
you do not think to think:
then it might happen that you sense
the mystery you have not explored
in the place you left,
something hidden behind doors,
something beyond
the reach of lights that you have missed.

Late Last Night

Late last night we drove through fog:
nothing but a vague onslaught at
the window: vapors, or was it breath?

the clouds of the earth coming at us
all along the road. In the watery
substance all turned the same:

lights around corners, dreams hidden
in rooms, the country wide as ocean,
the singleness in every name.

Irreconcilables

How to explain that on the day
we knew disease had invaded her
who had brought us into the world,
that death had conquered her like a weapon
she would not escape for long,
the winter sun spread vastly
and with utter ease
giving sharpness to each thing,
making all things stand out
as usually they don't:
a line of ships rooted like rocks,
and people in the frozen streets
free and light as breath
that clung to them like clouds.

Along the edge of the cold sky
a strip of deep lavender ran
like a streamer in a wind
pulled by an invisible string,

and the water in the port
made over by days of cold
looked chopped but permanent, as if
the sea were chunks of bottleglass.

And everywhere surfaces
giving off the winter sun
in a sort of game of catch,
throwing at each the light
that each received, so that
the effect was a jubilation,
a juggler's feat so fast,
so intricate a trick, the full

extent of its multifarious display
escaped our eyes. But the sense
that it was there, and that
it meant not to deceive
but to reveal a joy
did not elude us.

Yet we were driving to get to her
who we feared might soon be gone.
And how were we to reconcile
exuberance with what we were about?

That a car was taking us
to the condition we call death,
that extinction could occur
when the day showed itself
in a display so bright
it seemed a game of light,
that disappearance should
make sense when all about us
objects we could not name
flared up in a cold winter sun
and shone until we had to turn
from them as from a flame,
nothing in us could reconcile,
nothing in us could explain.

Enchanted Flowers

in memory of my mother

1.

She is a flower in the wind.
Her bloom is gone.
The wind must take her petals
one by one.
She brought joys to beholders,
stinging pain to intruders.
Lean stalk of a stem,
the wind once proud of her
now wails in and about her.
The seer cannot see herself.
Dying is the wind's full grief.

2.

Flute, flute
be your utmost!
A column of thin smoke
in that forever distant distance of
perpetual light.
Thin shape by flowers
entwined as though by a snake,
the mood of dancers
collected in a heap.
Flute, flute
till I weep!

3.

In total possession of themselves,
arrayed with every pollen, petal,
drinking insect each possessed;

arrived at their own enchantment,
arrived at last in that sphere
where storms do not enter,
where not they but the winds have died:
they hum to be thus collected,
humming absorb the anguish
of those about to cross over.

4.

Flow gently, flower.
Children once again,
we weep at your going,
weep for a reception
adequate for one such as you,
absorber of light,
bearer of our misjudgment.
You who pity us when,
returned to our purity
for the instant of your going,
we cannot endure it
and you break out
in renewed petals
in the air above our heads.

5.

Contained in the air
and spread across the distance
we take in in our days,
in the deep recesses of our beings
devoted to this enchantment,
striving to experience
flood of the scent
that pursues us: flowers
of numberless clouds, of wings
of wind falling toward each stem. . .

6.

You among the rare, the chosen ones
whose inner space is wind of scent,
do not insist on the attempt
to hold the bloom in trembling hands,
nor keep yourself from trying.
To stand straight, in the distance your eyes,
alert in sleep, in all your worldly ways
to hints and nuances that seek
the fragrance that you are:
is there any more to do
to honor flowers praising you?

7.

Who is alert is pious.
Imprints of things as they are
demolish notion and choice.
Who has the strength to replace
his will with the naturalness
of scented growth and death
touching body and eye,
glides across night and day,
is masterful, fragile as a bird:
exposed, exposed – alert!

8.

In separateness, transition's bitter mark,
an admixture of the space that gathered them
and the touch of red, of green, of violet
upon the cloudlike paleness of the frost
that curls to kill beneath each stem:
so do all move across the plain

assigned to each for our days.
What has been said is said again.
Of shadowy substance is the dance.
What's concrete is beyond such circumstance.

9.

In transition composed
the motion, pallor,
leaves of the rose.
In transition contained
the indwelling wind
that had languished once
on many a noble's parapet,
had lain within a flute,
had held upon a cheek
what to strong men is
a sign of the weak.

10.

But no! They are fools
who see and say it so.
Grandest of all,
as experience second to none,
flowers that fall from eyes
as response to
a more than human,
more than time-conditioned
circumstance.
Petals that rain
when the wind must come
to shake at a stem.
Gently, flow gently then:
flower, breathless, human.

1965

Wandlung

1.

Day after day, comes fall,
sky and sea are gray.
Along the coast, beneath bare boughs
there is the threat of ice.
Seasons of blossoms
and of dying leaves
have tumbled down streams
seething at the estuary
deprived now of summer stars
and of discoloring shades.

It is a time brisk and stark,
devoid of former flourishes.
The last of the south-going birds
have flown past
on to their separate seas.
Only the shrill warnings,
the questioning blares
of northern birds
spatter the air.
A few late leaves drift by.

2.

Down in the port
boats empty their registered cargo out
blurred in
the watery late autumnal haze
as if the bales were ghosts.
Boat after boat
or so the dampened foghorns say.

3.

Yearly, when summer's ease and fervor goes
young women mostly indoors,
young men in bars
have watery, melancholy eyes
that whisper of strangers
driving their horses up
uneven streets,
foreigners who whistle like winds
and sing.

Then will even the dogs lie low
so splendid, so rare—
and yet not surprising
almost in fact anticipated
as if expected year after year—
so commanding the sight
of the bright strangers
driving their black
wet horses
up the hill.

Some Elements of Drama

The Scene: A Bathing Resort on Spain's Costa Brava

A dark mist hangs upon the sea.
The change in sky is out of character,
and the weird behavior of the water.
Upset the summer guests walk up
and down as if expecting news.

Large birds not common in these parts
are perched on tops of cliffs
where on more ordinary days
the bathers sit to dry. To relieve
this mood, the owners of
hotels have put on jazz.

A table-umbrella torn from
its metal stand, turned inside-out
by an abnormal wind
lies unretrieved
like a disaster out of reach,
threateningly distorted
on a shunned, a battered beach.

What has happened?
What monster has broken forth
out of some vengeful mind
to pursue its ghastly design?
What ill-distorted shape
that stalks now on the sea,
hissing behind the air,
driving the waves, fist
upraised, clouding
the minds of men like mist?

No one can tell
the happening beneath
the fury and the lifting fronts
of sea, how long this turn
will last, and what
will be revealed
when the disturbance ends.

Silently the strange large birds
sit perched on cliffs.
Their seeing eyes are sealed.

Encounter at Tehuixtla

A sulphur spring in Mexico

He was a farmhand, a youth
bringing freshness, innocence
to his beginning adult years,
coyly as a newly planted tree
in its first spring. Or so
it seemed to the two Europeans—
one still young enough to be
his older friend, the other
old enough to be his mother—
who had spotted him
among a truckload of laborers
come for a quick swim.

He was equally drawn to them,
would not take his eyes off them
as if he were watching a film.
"City people must excite him,"
reasoned the Europeans, "particularly
if foreign and he feels
he is in turn exciting them."
Which he was, whom they
had hoped to come across
in their flights around the world.
The Europeans had long ago
envisioned him, young,

primitive and handsome,
coming out of the sea,
or at mountain resorts
in the rapid drift of early mist.
Now in Mexico, miles from
the nearest town, he stood

in front of them ready to bathe,
his farmhand's clothes dropped
where he was, his body fixed
on them. "His gaze," one of
the two said in French,
"could not be more charming."

"Like that of a slender deer,"
the other replied, "an animal
hiding behind a tree
looking out upon the field
with eyes trusting but wary,
dark and shaped like chestnuts."
"Yes, but don't you see in him as well
the fire of a rose
seeking to outdo itself in all its beauty
and be possessed
before this quickest spell
of total flowering goes?"

And mixed with that, both agreed
they saw him also as a girl,
a gentle creature in
a simple dress at church,
or at a crossroad on her knees
before her saint, or at her
lover's bed offering flowers
of the field, cornflowers perhaps,
and without uttering a sound
making it quite clear
it was body and heart
that she had brought.

But as the slender Mexican
who was indeed built like

a tender god, to impress
the foreigners threw himself
into the sulphur pool
and let himself be drawn
into the seething spring,
water pulling into its
whirlpool nest all manner
of things that came along,
whether they could take
the crashing force or not,

and as the Europeans saw him
fight this element with ease
as though in his upraised fist
he held an invisible spear,
he might have been a figure
out of some myth riding the water
as if it were a beast.
And what he showed them was this:
that he was a spirit in the flesh
eager to jest with the yield
and turmoil of the earth.
Seeing him thus, the world travelers

revised their impression of him.
Handsome he was, and primitive
and young, but also strong
not frail and vague like some wreathed
youth risen from out of the past.
When they drove off as if
to flee their thoughts, they did
not find him by the road
looking at them as they had
envisioned him, his sad eyes
saying many unsaid things.

Instead, for a distance out
they heard the laughter of the men
he had come with for a swim.

Lament for a Talent

Whatever it was that gave
you radiant stillness like
a fluttering air, is gone.
You were the recipient once,
were the figure that seemed to walk
like someone wrapped in light
across an agitated bay or lake.
You could not accept
the apparition was
for our sake, not yours,
could not give yourself
to it enough to become
the radiance you were possessed of.
Now emptied of what
is so much bigger than you are,
you stumble on,
err, err,
a rower without oars,
and are off course
no matter where you are.

The Mist from Tree to Tree

They seemed this morning on their way to work
not mindful of the fog they could not see,
not mindful of an eye hidden somewhere,
the sign on someone rushing by,
the mist from tree to tree.

They hurried on.
They reached their destination one by one.
The eye looked on
when they went in, when they came out.
Heading homeward on a darkening road
a fog closed in. Someone was lifted, carried.

Gentle Lamb

At a street corner
waiting to cross: two boys.
Pressed against the chest of one
a dog slender as a greyhound,
timid as a lamb.

Traffic is heavy,
the boys are waiting for
a path to form.
Here in midtown New York
on a gray winter day,

they are a vision dimmed
in most, are the dream
flowing through their eyes and skin—
fire on this frost-
and world-encrusted ground.

And like a flare
sustained and surrounded by air,
the dog enfolded by
the boy's arm
rests on a tenderness

the boy is himself
seeking to express,
a tenderness before which he—
also at home in
an invisible mantle
that clings to him,

gentle as a lamb—
is himself dumb

as the animal
he carries in his arm.

Today's Troubadours

Troubadours in modern dress
lack luster of the hearth.
In absence of fortified tower,
glow in window toward which
innocent hearts aspire,
in lieu of idealized love
what are singers singing of?

The shadow of themselves
on horseback in twos,
ramshackle walls in view.
The feel of their loneliness
expressed by untamed land
and lonely, lawless place.
Immersed thus with themselves,

with their restlessness,
their stance is not romance
but awkwardness. Gone from them,
for a time at least, the song of praise
that gave many a troubadour
distinction for his lines
and splendor to his face.

The Unworldliness That He Creates

1.

Alien in environments he has come to for the first time,
he is nevertheless at home in the eyes of those who look
upon the strangeness he creates,

is at home on streetcorners he chances on
where men stand about discussing events of which he knows nothing,

is at home along the boulevards where the big hotels are,

in the parks at night when the crowds have left,

in the garden where on Sunday mornings there is music of swans,
of peasant maidens lost to madness out of love,

is at home in these as a bird is above hillsides and towns touched on for
the first time.

2.

As a face becomes real when contained in a surface that reflects,
as the soul has an inkling of what it can be
when received in the eyes of a stranger,

what among the things that depend upon
reception by the heart
is comparable to the recognition that

the flutter of wild ducks, the cry
of wild ducks whose object of pursuit
the observer cannot trace—only the cry
pierces the park as if despair
had been sounded on a trumpet—

that such happenings one mild afternoon
in a garden of a major capital,

that the aloofness of a swan, its utter lack of agitation,

that these suggest the cold majesty, the grave
beauty of total self-concern?

That these cries, these calls, these cruel attitudes and gestures,

that the young man lying in the grass his face resting in one hand

that the old woman sitting under a dark tree,

that both, and countless more
letting what goes on around them go by them as if
the cry of ducks, the target lost behind shadows,
the poise of the swan, and the anguish,
the reception in the stranger's heart

were no more than a slight wind touching the leaves,
no more than clouds drifting by,
no more than the mild shadow of clouds. . .

To recognize that these are no more than a slight wind touching the leaves;

to recognize that to experience these,
to let them be like a final phrase—
name, place, days, years chiseled roughly in rough stone—

to let them be part of the heart's reception means

they have achieved themselves

and having achieved themselves have become less than formless

a thing for which there is no word
for it has not the shape of any thing

and received rests there as that,
as that without change. . . .

3.

Who is he upon whom those who see him as a stranger look as
one looks upon someone who suggests a world at once foreign and
intimate, a world that though distant reveals something one cannot
quite visualize but has yearned for, has said its name and responded
with tenderness. . .

who is he upon whom those who take him as a stranger look and
are amazed, for he recognizes himself in the eyes of those he does not
know, who all at once and for a moment they cannot explain or even
remember, know him, and are astonished as they have been when
absorbed in the rarest of artworks, love words, songs of dreams. . .

who is he in whom the things he looks upon achieve themselves?
He in whom their forms are released and become the essence that he
is, and is theirs?

Who is he who stands before a painting in which the mother weeps,
and the father weeps, and the son has suffered all there is to be suffered?

Who is he who stands before this painting, and weeps?

4.

Whether he stands before a canvas whereon man's ultimate condition
is expressed through the most gentle, the most beautiful body possible,

whether he sits on a bench on a Sunday
and receives in his eyes the light
and in his arms the flesh of the candles
the women that pass him have lit
out of love for their husbands
devotion to their children and duty to parents
in the churches they have left,

and receives as well the songs they intended
the ones joined in
and the ones that shook their bodies
as they knelt or stood against a pillar
and the thought of a loved one who had come and gone
bolted through them,

and receives also the looks and songs of the men
on the day away from their routine involvement.

On the horizon the boats they will not cease to construct.

Out of the waves, out of the sky
eyes into which they can continue to look

eyes that will return to them what they had wanted to see

eyes that will make them what they had wanted to become

the look that will give them what they had or should have had

the look that will wash away the darkness that had troubled them

will lift them to their rightful place
and make them what they are.

They bow their heads,
in the evening pick up guitars for their songs of fate.

They weep over they know not what.
                                        Except that
though it may be nameless, it is closer to them
than the wind of the sea on their faces
and the light of midnight on their hair.

And infinite the shapes, the forms of tenderness
their yearning takes

The expressed of the expression is always Love
Love itself hath said

and the shapes that rise in their hearts and are dimmed in their eyes
are all as gentle, as beautiful as that body of love
that died and dies for love. . .

And receives this, the possibilities inside them,
their mostly unexpressed intention, the quality
that pours from them as though their bodies were a watery cloth
wrapped loosely around the quickest, brightest light,

as they stroll by him,
point a hand in his direction though they may be engaged in
conversation or may sit around a sidewalk table discussing events of
which he knows nothing

although at times they may look at him directly

and he is not there

only the look they seek
the eyes they know

the worship that is theirs:

the sign in the sky
the sails they construct.

5.

He in whom the pain in extremity is received and released

who is outside extremity or its pain could not be endured

he is not man, not woman,
he is not this, not that,
not I, not he, not you.

Movement transformed into art is an attempt to show this:

that form is so multifaceted it cannot be solid.
That color can only suggest color
and that color, movement and light
can only approximate
the quality the eye cannot behold,
the ear not catch,
the hand not endure.

And he who becomes he in the eyes of others,
who is alien regardless of the intimacy with which he receives
the streets he walks on for the first time,

he who is stranger to those who marvel at the foreign way
in which he moves—his ease as though gliding—

is it any wonder that when he comes into a street

when he sits on a bench or stands before a painting,

when the sky trembles in his eyes,

that he weeps?
                       For what is he but response?

And he flows into that which flows into him as a wave into the sea

and the sea into waves
and both are water,
both are one.

6.

Festive the crowds the evening before a day of celebration in the
square that was once first in the city and is now famed for its age,
style, agreeable proportions, and the equestrian statue of a king in its
center.

Tomorrow they will go to the pools, will sing on the roads, will lie
on slopes, will eat on terraces overlooking gorges, rivers, celebrated
bridges, aqueducts, historic sites; in the evening will follow sugges-
tions of love through crowded streets and squares with tall fountains
whose faint spray the air carries.

They have draped flags around the balconies, there are candles on all
tables of the restaurant fenced in by boxed hedges, and many the lan-
guages among the people who dine; those who are local stroll in
groups under the arcades, and the places where people eat and drink
standing up are crowded.
Is it because it is nevertheless the time when separateness comes into
its own, distinct as a shadow in front or beside one, that he turns
from these, runs from waiters, from the clatter of food being served,
from drifts of conversations?

Is it because it is the time when those to whom streets and squares
and the names of the flowers that look odd in the night along the
coast are known in a language he cannot speak, are strangers as he is,
the night before a celebration, each alone in the darkness?

In the taxi, back to the part of the city where the hotels are

and elsewhere and later
down the broad road that runs along the coast,
he does not resist it, lets it possess him:

the demands of the night in a land that is alien—

and walks into the air to be near the fountains
and feels on his hands and face the spray that the air carries

and elsewhere and later
takes into himself all that the light of the moon on a
      restless sea is suggestive of. . .

7.

When it is time to leave,
though he was alien where he has been,
and to those in whose language he cannot answer,
and to those who do not feel in him the possibilities in man
and the background he reflects, is alien still:

he knows that he has been at home.

In paintings, the folds of rich garments, the dove that hovered,
the movement of figures upward, spearlike, flamelike as a prayer;

in the eyes of those who passed by him, sat near him,
who said much of themselves though not a word was said:

firm glimmers, kindling suggestions of what he knows best
rose to his demands and needs as waves to stormy wind.

As if on a stool near the chair of one through whom
birds roar, flowers sway, generations sing a tale—
from whom silence rises like a sword in flames—
attentive to murmurs that follow once the word was said
(what child has not experienced this?)

he knows he will be what those around him are

who will be what he is

and that they live not only in their songs and dreams
but also in the things they make—
things that retain their human presence like a hush—
and when he leaves
                              receives their looks
their flames in paintings
not as farewell
but beckoning, acknowledging wave. . .

and where he sat and walked

wherever there were those who looked upon the unworldliness that
                              he creates

all that is air remembers him.

Madrid, Lisbon, Cascais

Short Poem

When eyes pass by trembling with presence,
hold on to the urge for possession of
the love without which you must learn
to remain content; then love with all you possess
that shadow wherein hovers a promise
like a young swallow in a thicket of trees.

Costa do Sol

Even the soil is at home
along coasts where men unload
each night from boats
fish they have caught,
and in a dark street
a woman sings of
the death of love,
of youth that must burn,
of fate that must come.

The Poem

Out of continued striving
have I fashioned this.
Out of the indefinable,
its attentiveness,
yes, its embrace.

But I must add:
cold collisions,
humming, humming,
and an empty bed.

Unalterables

Mistakes are dredged up again,
not mine but before mine began,
of figures I never knew,
and those I did know gone,
except that since what had
been done to them is carried on
through me, they lurk about,
unwelcome presences unseen
but evident like something

moving beneath dead leaves.
I thought I was done with them.
What need had I of faceless creatures,
agitation in their hair,
uttering unalterables
in languages I refused to hear?
Other sayings filled my ears,
other directions shook me—signs
that led to gates and guards who kept

the doom-promoters out. I realized
when I returned that doom or past
were unthinkable behind those gates,
but learned that they come back,
figures of my old mistakes,
who in spite of where I have been,
what I have found and seen,
want me to dance with them
their old, disordered dance.

The Statue

For years I've tried to destroy
the statue in myself: baroque
façades I stood in front of
as a boy, strict rows of trees,
columns, fountains, pavilions,
sights meant for royal ease.

For harmony's sake I've tried
to rid myself of rigid
aspects. It's just as well
I don't succeed!
Someone departs, someone is wounded.
A woman runs across a street

her hands lifted in lament,
a grieving man walks from
a house with lowered head.
At moments such as these,
when pain runs through the body
and tensions flicker in a nervous sky,

the statue in a shadowed lane—
like a figure when a storm is gone—
breaks through in me, comes forth again:
and I observe with stone-
like eye, the dying
of what is meant to die.

Sleep Took Me Far

Sleep took me far, so far
a force that works for wakefulness
came to demand me back.
Caught without will, used by it
as weather does a stone or metal thing
for driving wind and snow through it,
I was pulled from that depth
where life's true countenance
might show itself in starkness,
instill in me its awe,
by a wind furious at my door.

And followed as I was led,
and woke because I lacked the strength
to say: "Though what in
your turbulence you hold
are worldly possibilities to which
much in me clings; though mind and will
be faded into sleep
and you have caught me unawares,
in the name of nothing less
than all the entity I am,
I say: Away!   away! . . . "

Worldliness

Worldliness is your enemy.
Never think otherwise.
It does not tolerate for long
love that you love.
From where the pure lament
played on ancient instruments?
To what is a sob a response?
Trumpets lift our spirits up. To where?
The world is entangled with
continued decay and death.
It courts but abhors
the opposite it needs.
Entrapped in its laws
it ravages love,
hacks at truth,
weeping, weeping it must do
what is incumbent upon it to do!

How moving to think
that from time to time
a white horse does come
bringing a redeemer in human form.

Rocky Tarn

Fog hung above the lake.
A giant web of mist.
We sat on a screened-in porch.
There was talk of history,
of civilization's need
for inwardness.
Tall trees surrounded us,
in the dampness looking like
soggy, dark birds of unnatural size
whose eyes are shut,
wings half-closed.
This then is inwardness:
to see blurred nothingness
close in upon a lake,
to make comparisons but know
they do not hold,
are meaningless—
in the depth of sleep
where man arises,
takes his arrow,
mounts his steed.

The Ship

An Evening Elegy

1.

Small swallows chirping joyously
swirl about the town's belfries and rooftops,
fly in circles above Dubrovnik's bay
as the sun sets. Slowly, slowly
this far south, the sky's red pales,
the heat of the day subsides,
slowly the whiteness comes,
the pale time when outlines are less distinct,
stillness descends and churches ring.

A boat making a wide arc
heads for the town's small port.
From my balcony I see the boat not as
a craft ferrying summer crowds to island beaches,
bringing peasants to the markets of this town,
but as a slender ship plying its course in a haze,
making its way across my mind
as the hours reach the day's white time.

Words repeat themselves inside my head:
Objects of yearning have made
the human being the overwhelmed
inheritor
        Soon
the long evening will start, whiteness
set in. The fiery time is done.

2.

The ship I see behind the haze
is white, long, yachtlike;

stewards bring trays, officers
are dressed in the best of uniforms.
Tapestries hang in the lounge,
the chandeliers are dimly lit.
I see myself standing toward the bow
looking out into the foggy sea.
Where have we not been, what have we not seen?
The Vienna of my childhood falling, towers,
palaces, museums, parks and lilac gardens
swept up by the waves. The face of the woman
struggling to reach me is that of
my mother calling, but the waters
have come between us. What was
is nothing now. Even those shadows
I went at night in pursuit of—
figures that had run from my dreams—
are drenched by the waves, their features
blurred and often repellent.
What once tempted, as though concealed in the face
were the truth of an angel, has altered
its visage. Or I have grown indifferent
and can no longer see
what once I thought I saw.

The ship has passed through the time of the fire.
Whiteness sets in and I do not think
I am ready to meet it,

do not think I am ready for
the obliterating sameness it brings.

Objects of yearning have made
the human being the overwhelmed
inheritor

Where the ship comes from, or where it is going,
who has answered what many have asked?
And who could grasp the total meaning
conveyed by the look, the nod, the silence,
the words of the few who did get to
where questions are not, and became
the inspiration of civilizations and of cities?

Is it from out of these stirrings and tensions,
and because of the sacred glimpses that stand out in
the landscape of human experience like glaciers,
like monumental structures made of the whitest of rock—

is it from and because of these
that the yearning has risen,
that the ship has set forth on its way,
has passed by man's greatest expressions of faith and of striving:
pyramids and colonnades,
arenas of worship and theatres,
stairways, parks, palaces,
statues, fountains and hedges along waterways?

And from the walls
the silent faces of ancestors,
of kings, of saints,
and along the walls
gilded chairs, music racks,
a harp, a harpsichord. . .

Water falls from the ship as it goes,
water that is the ship's sole course

Objects of yearning have made
the human being the overwhelmed
inheritor

4.

And as part of the process,
part of the span the ship crosses:
I have gone and returned
and have gone again,
have yearned, have reached,
have torn at the mystery
like veils from the face,
have taken the forbidden body in my arms,
and what should I reach for again
and where?

Can the day yield any more than
the sight of windows blazing,
giving off an almost blinding fire
from the water as the sun goes down?
Can I repeat what I had caught
in the shade of the alleys
when the clock struck noon, struck four
and the drapes were drawn?
The figures that stole from my rooms
while I drifted through sleep like a ship,
can they be summoned again who are gone?
And if they returned
would they have hollows for eyes,
seaweed for hair?
and their bodies the pallor of the drowned?

Objects of yearning have made
the human being the overwhelmed
inheritor

5.

All things throughout the day
are separate and distinct.
When day goes, when outlines fuse
and the past falls off,
when desires float by
like scraps from far away:
a substance that contains all these
breaks forth. Flames will come again,
but whiteness rules when they are gone.

Evening lights ablaze in windows
fade out into the sea, and our dreams mix with
the waters' even flow, but behind these
where all is the same,
where nothing changes
are we not as we have always been?
Is it not because of this,
because of whiteness
that our thoughts and feelings are aflame?

White, white, center of fire, white at the core!

Whiteness at the end of flights and flights of stairs!

Cloud, wool of the lamb, gaze of the animal and saint
above the heights of trees and the pillars' stone!

*Objects of yearning have made
the human being the overwhelmed
inheritor*

1969

Two Poems on the Firebird

I - Gift of the Firebird

I will give you what you need.
Though I tremble, I am not weak.
What causes me to flutter
does not end. Free is what I am,
and you must let me free.
Who am I? The fire of my feathers,
my flaming presence only tells in part.
No one beholds all of what I am.
I may be in your eye and heart
but I am never owned.
No arms enfold me for long.
I yield so you will let me go.
Know though that my appearance here
in the shadow of golden fruit
shall not be in vain. My gift,
this fiery feather will remind you
you have held what you shall miss:
it will slay falsehoods and mists,
will free you from the grip of those
whose trickery does not live
unless you take it to be true.

II - Addressed to the Firebird

Ever since I held you in my arms
(a flaming presence as I knew afterwards)
what is unclear and ill-intended,
the murky force that thrives on refuse,
has been dispelled. All is now in place,
pale in pure light, each rising to its
full height and worth. All I

have done has flourished into fame:
but what is order, what is gain to me
who am bound to you, my bird of fire?

As time is piled on me like frost on leaves,
wherever I go, whatever I look at
it is our meeting I relive as in a haze:
I am young, you are under a tree
of golden fruit; I have stumbled on
your garden by mistake, or so I think;
I catch you, hold you; clasped in a dance
I demand, you yield; I entreat, you elude
being both coldness of a swan
and passion of a bird aflame;
too much nearness, my senses lost,

I let you go. Since then your gift—
this fiery feather I am left with,
your promise in my mind and heart—
has brought health where withering was,
success in skills I wanted most.
But what is order, what is gain to me
who am bound to you in no more than memory?
To have held you once should be enough,
but it is not: consumed by your flame—
a yearning beyond any worldly desire—
consuming me too slowly, too slowly,
my cruel bird of fire!

Perspectives

1.

The agitation in and on the land,
the indifferent calm of space beyond:
these two perspectives do not meet.
Both extend from man, extend from him
like roots and branches from a tree.
Each nudges him differently.
One demands his arms, his legs;
the other, of his head and heart,
makes no claim unless sought out,
is the far-off point of his return
where nothing ever moves away,
and all he wants and does
is approved of and endorsed.
Though both are his, they are opposed:
the two directions do not meet.

2.

Small birds, dark birds, birds of
the night nestling in
his hair (how shall he rest?),
whispers of a love wild as flames
lead him here, command him there:
"What have you arms and legs for?
And the milk of the male,
the power underneath your skin?
Remember this, remember this:
from now on years—
one, or ten, or more—
go quicker than before!"
Not the age-old dream nor even lust,

fright drives him out into
the nervous stillness of the moon-thick night.

3.

The indifferent space about his head,
the distances where towers rise,
gold glimmers at the end of sight,
the perspective too supreme
to attract attention to itself:
it does not beckon, does not nag him
as the one that depends upon
his arms, his legs, his skin.
And yet, pulled into
the agitation in and on the land
at night and in the day, it is
the other perspective he cannot forget,
that kinder aspect in himself
as detached from the needs
he is yet forced to meet, as are
the things that fly, from earth.

History

What do we know of what is behind us?
The old town we drove through yesterday
is as remote from us now
as the century it was built,
water covering all our yesterdays equally.

What do we know of what lies ahead?
We see the old inns coming toward us,
white irregular walls, windows spaced unevenly,
women and children waiting at corners to cross.
We see the end of the town and the fields and forests beyond it,
but also hear the water waiting to cover them as we pass.

And what do we know
of what we do not see,
of what neither moves toward us
nor falls into watery wastes as we pass?

Old Coat

Years have gone by, forty and some,
and I am suddenly aware
they have. The pangs, the feeling
that the marvelous exists somewhere
and that what I really am is in
the yearning most men are not conscious of—
for that horse in embroidered cloth
trotting with lowered mane
toward that bright tower out of sight—
all of that, all of that is just the same.

I see an Emperor on stage.
He is dressed in the blue of skies,
a stiff glove is on one hand,
bow and arrow in the other.
Falcon, it seems to me he cries,
Falcon you led me to my fondest wish;
withered is all, ashes my hunt
now your red wing is gone!
Falcon, my falcon, return!
Away from him I am
his language hard to discern,
the torment in his face,
the agony of his distress.
None of this has changed.
But years have gone.
I have sat in rooms
radiant, ablaze, way out and out of sight.

I returned dragging an old coat behind,

black blotch on the floor,
old shadow dark as blindness and failure,

a coat handed down, a coat
I have not the strength to throw away:
mantle that in the end is all
the gorgeously attired fighter has
to protect him in battle
and cover his death. Years
have not dissolved this ancient shield, the skin—
though it wears out in spots
I am obliged to mend, or have it done.
                              Old women

chant on   chant on
as practiced fingers sew.

India

I sit before an urn—
actually a monument
with a cavity wherein
the urn is kept.
Camphor burns, a handful
of incense sticks.
A few men and women
stand with folded hands
and chant a sacred name.
Nearby a river flows.
Palms sway, birds call.

Though I sit before
ashes kept in a monument
in a compound with a name,
in a village with a name,
in a country, continent with
a name, I have no name for
the cavity wherein I sit
withdrawn, withdrawn—
where visibles thaw out,
rivers dry up
and unknown winged creatures
hum, flap, shout.

Unnatural Heat, Moosehead Lake

Night. All is still. No wind, not a breath
of air. The lake, heavy and compliant,
lies without moving like a dog
exhausted in the heat.
The raccoons that sniff for food
when it is dark have not come out;
they lie somewhere as though drugged,
nothing but motionless heaps of fur
on the hot, the suffering earth.
No human breath but mine, and nothing stirs.

I lie naked on my bed,
the sheet thrown back,
and with the waiting night and earth
I wait. Nothing is close to me now but
my needing, my tormented flesh.
It is a moment of unnaturalness
and my long familiar tormentors—
shapes that speak of need, of lust, of emptiness—
seize the moment for their taunts
and torturing address.

They grin at me as if to say:
you thought you'd conquered us!
Conceited, you believed you'd
be unmoved as a rock,
that only angels would appear
to lift you from your deep distress
when in and around you there is
nothing but the worst of heat,
and that sick longing on your face!
Which we are! For what we are, what we are

is this! They say, grin and move toward me
out from every dark recess.
No wind is there, no air
but they who make no noise,
who do not breathe, who have
horns for crowns, hooves
for feet, they whose lust
is animal, whose perfect limbs are
of human shape, are everywhere,
everywhere their taunts, their stare.

Dead, as though dead
the lake, nothing stirs in it.
A hot moon has spilled itself into it.
Naked, I lie waiting on my naked bed.
The body's tormentors
are closing in on it.

Words of the Pilgrim

Nothing matters to me but
inner accord.
Come, beasts,
I'll face you if I must.
I'll walk through the dark with
the unfulfilled, the lost.
Let their terror be my cry.
What is hidden
shall come forth.
Light insists
nothing shall be missed.

The Tenuous Line

Listen now, listen to this:
the line you must hold on to
is tenuous, but it is all
you have to help you on.
You cannot for a moment forget
where you have been,
and what and where it is
you must clear the way
to reach.

You are not Theseus
but you too must have combat with
shapes half human and half beast.
All your desires must be faced,
and your desire for
the beautiful—to dally,
be entangled with
the deeply sensual—
leads you to this.

Unlike Ariadne I take
no girlish interest in you.
But to get to where you are going
you must defeat
what breaks out on the way.
And this you cannot do
without impersonal aid.
My voice you must learn
to listen to,

the tenuous line, to see.
The curious fact of this
your labyrinthian path is:
there is not one desire,

not one nagging call
that lingers in your dreams
that you shall miss.
What you have asked for
you shall have: triumphal

visits with cities of
the past; exchanges
on flowerbeds with
compelling seekers of the night;
tears on sensitive faces
in response to
what you are, what you,
by saying, by a
lament, a smile, have hinted at.

You will not be denied any
of this, but this:
what you hold you will not keep.
Applause you will not assume
as yours. Like this thread
you will not be attached
to any of what
lies on your path—
unless, of course, unless. . .

Your gain will be in other ways.
Besieged, you will not shun
the hateful looks, the trumpet
blares, the outraged cries.
At dawn, you will hold
perfection on your eyes.
You will not say: "I've had
enough, have had my fill"
but will ask to move on, move on—
until, of course, until. . .

The Look Back

From you
I ask this simple act:
look back at me as if
recollecting your whole life
and most of all
your deepest wants.
Look back at me in a way
that will let me look at you
as if in our eyes
fortifications dissolved to dust
and dust into space. Look at me

as if to say, Now I have
looked into myself.
Symbols of timelessness,
stone trimmings, stone heads and stares,
powerful embodiments, drift there
as in watery surfaces—
lamplights that lead us back
into a past that is.
Only by feeling close to that
which we can never reach
but lasts are we
enlarged and comforted.

1975

Les Nuits d'Été

The soul yearns for trees
rustling on summer nights,
for bays where are reflected
windows, faces that hesitate
to do more than suggest
feelings that brought them to the ledge.

The soul yearns for recognition.
To declare what cannot be said
is not its agitation.
To be received, to let its wings
be felt like a bird in its
ample cage where beautifully,

sorrowfully it sings.
To be denied its own reflection
is the soul's relentless grief.
Not to be acknowledged,
not understood—be it
in towns, by the sea,
in shimmering woods.

Enough

Enough! Let this season end,
this summer of unnatural heat,
of untimely storms,
of water subject to winds,
of land subject to
nature's whims, aridity of
human imprint: phantoms
whose eyes speak of
wasted lives, journeys left,
loves not had, lusts

not tried; phantoms
in place of flesh
and passion in the night. Enough!
Enough of nature's wiles
and torments of
the solitary mind.
Give me the human touch and need. . .
Give me the great structures in the mist. . .
the hand held out,
the far-off lines that feed and feed.

Continuity

Shades go with me where I go.
In dreams they perform
in various guises
their accusations,
failed enterprises,
make of their own
thwarted ambition
my life, their mission.

The path ahead of me
they've marked, have put
the faces there that I must meet,
have lit the halls, kept dark the street,
have hidden all but what I need
to find on my own
where they too would have gone.

Who are with me as I reach
the door; who move into
my hands, my fingers on the knob:
as I come to take
and attempt to hold
what for them was merely foretold.

The Hand upon His Head

1.

Of where he has been he now steadily partakes.
He may not have evidence of this
as one has of sensory things,
but that he has been there,
that no occurrence could equal it,
before or after, that he knows.
Heaven on earth. Above trees birds suspended,
clouds do not move—earth as heaven—
and man sits there as if his worldly being
had left him, and a white presence
had cast itself across him like a shade.

If they ask him where he has been
he cannot say. But they sense it,
see in him what they imagined they
themselves would one day be,

see him as someone they might encounter on
a dusty road, all at once like an apparition
as if he had stepped from the hazy distance,
from the heat of the air.

2.

Waters he sailed across, the secluded
courts he left behind, acres of uplands
aglow in the sun's haze as though held
in a dust of gold, jasmine and lotus
petals in bowls, the girlish calf
and peacock behind a wall of shrubs:

these he no longer thinks about.
Traces fade and the water flows.
It is the waters' roar in the heart
he knew, the shapes then
wet and glistening.

Yet when he wakes and starts the day,
when he lies down and he is like a man
about to enter a grotto in his boat:
it is from *there* he comes,
it is to *there* he goes. This he knows.

★   ★   ★

3.

Of the two continents he now moves between,
one, the result of departure,
is not only devoid of
the essence of where he was and is,
it has been untouched by it as a land
toward which the water flows but does not reach.
The other was reached, was drenched,
and the residue is there still:

in dark corners of castles and homes,
in the ruins and ancient stones—
the scraps of walls by the sea—
in people he meets
where they have come, along the coast,
to step out of their daily routine
into long nurtured, over centuries developed
cherished aspects of themselves:
their ambition for a life they cannot even name,
the beholding of themselves, as in a flash, in all perfection.

They lie in the sun, they watch each other sitting on rocks,
the tempters and the tempted; at night
they sit on chairs in rows or on stone stairs
and do not move. A great singer is expressing what
without knowing, they have always known:

deep within themselves lies the truth
of what they are.
                        Heavy waters pound upon the door.
All at once they feel they understand.
The residue of centuries is in their eyes.
They applaud to say
what they could never say in words,
and then they leave.

4.

Though he knows that what they are today
and what lies in them as residue
no longer connects, it is
that residue that gives him strength
and in their midst feels himself
in place, revived, and satisfied.

Among them he can be himself, can hoist up,
bring up his deepest wants
and live them for a while. And it is important
this be done. A flag over a camp, vast lands,
announces a country's dominance.
The personal self brought up, freed,
declares this conquest: to allow
the terrains, the crevices to be filled;
to open one's being
so the waters may flow.

5.

At–homeness in the soil
is an accumulation of presences
that tie the living to their land
like a floating garment tied to the body wearing it.

There it is that wounds can open up,
a scream erupt like a birth

where paths break out into halls and ponds

where desires can meet themselves in bodies moving past

where as evening falls
an alto sings
and like hooded monks the shapes of the flickering wind
the candles have cast on the walls.

6.

In an atmosphere like this,
amid accumulations such as these,
what is there of what is human that cannot be received?

And he lies on the rocks in the sun
and walks at night by the sea below
cypresses, palms, oleander in bloom,
and all that he ever dreamed of as personal love
is now at his arm's touch in the dark

and having been where he was,
and being rooted there toward where flow all his thoughts,
he lets free his innermost wants of love

and suffers them

suffers them as only he in whom the past is free
can suffer.

7.

This, even they—there—no longer see:

that it is not enough to provide more for most

that the door must be kept ajar

that no real guests are there where there is not the proper host

that bread has meaning only when it dissolves

that without processionals, recessionals, preludes and fugues played
                                        high above crowds

that without ceremonial robes, dim lights
and the diffusing effects of sacred smoke:
there can be no repose.

The impulse that has made them what they are—

and of their world a place in which they are at home—

is with them still

but, their interests diverted by now,
access to it is lost.
                    To reach it—
for how could they not want it
seeing what came out of it all around them

in churches, palaces, portraits, parks?—
and aware still of its inaudible, alluring call
some among them seek out dark avenues for their need,
linger about, their eyes
quick as animals, their tongues
for the moment mute.

What would they make of him seeing him there?
For where men come together out of yearning—
their deep, never fully comprehended need—
their desires draw him there as well.

8.

Because his place is now across the sea
he must in time depart
for the shores that have meant
departure for all who settled there
and arrives knowing once again
departure to be an alien state,

recognition a need
again to be pursued

intimacy a quality deep and reflecting as
a corridor with mirrors on all sides,

and knows that although
of where he has been
he steadily partakes

that there across the sea
he is nowhere as at home
as on his quest:

figures he meets on its path,
music he hears,
landscapes he sees there
return him to
where he has never left—

that room of his true return

the very core of intimacy,
the hand upon his head.

★   ★   ★

9. Afterword

Who can claim him or what he represents?
He cannot therefore be talked of as "I".
Even those select ones in whom he lives,
through whom is continued the impulse that he is,
even they, compounded of him, see him
apart from them, ahead of them always.

He is like the armor, the suit of conquests
that awaits them, and they, they are
the timid, the frightened ones forced from
their homes, from roles in the world
they could never assume, charged to
discover distances, to surmount ancient barriers,
all for the glory of their departed home.

He is at once their ideal, distant from them,
and the voice that commands them, though not
by words, the cause of their passage, the throb
in their being that spurs them on:
and he it is, he in them, who goes.

It is he, he in me, moved to weep
when children gather, the organ is played
and people strolling look in at open doors;
when a great singer has sung of
the anguish of youth, the dance of death;

when I express my love of place, of the
accumulated time and shadows of trees,
of regal homes it holds
through the one I love
and think of it afterward
in another, a distant house:

how I went up the stairs as the light broke
and left my love alone in the bed
covered by sleep, a moment glittering
like the water outside in the canal.

He stands ahead of me, not always facing me
and I must make my way toward him.

I carry out, attempt to carry out, nothing else.

HE is the instigator
                                      HE

my response

Two Poems on the Same Figure

1. Phrase Retrieved From Dream

He looks free as a dove-catcher
she said, recognizing in him
qualities she knew she would understand only
when facing them. The other woman,
attending him, accepted what was said
as if accustomed to hear him spoken of as
the center where disparate opposites meet
or spurt forth from like fountain jets.
The catcher of what was free and yet
not free from being caught by him.

2. Who Is He

Behind me silent figures stand
in wide-rimmed hats, their faces
blank. I do not know what to do
to make them go away.
They keep me from the world that lies ahead.
They keep me from the world of the dead.
Tears run down my face.
I do not know what I must do.
I dream of my parents as grand actors
and of the line of admirers
waiting to express their debt.
Tears run down my face
and I see a small Hindu
bare to the waist
bending at the river's edge
and filling his small tin cup.

Who is He

who made them go away?
Who is He
who took my tears
and filled His cup?

Frail Perfection

Swan,
I come upon your name in a book
and there you are in front of me
in many places, various poses.
It's said you are malicious, bite
mercilessly when interfered with
as you glide, stop, your wings
lifted up, the stream rushing down
into your tree-bordered lake
hangs glistening in the air,
and something, something rustles there.

Those who've heard you cry then say
it is a sound out-of-joint,
a blare of malice, of nasty despair.
But at the sight of your name in a book
I see you not as your own nature would

describe you but only as
your beauty suggests, in the midst of
a cultivation you symbolize:
clouds, hanging branches, reflective faces,
all shimmering as you glide and glide.

Coming upon your name in a book
I hear the music to which dancers
imitate your movements and
response, your fluttering as
something rustles through the trees
and water glistens in the air:
Swan,
you are this outline in my mind
of frail perfection.

On Behalf of Orpheus

Furies, let the singer pass!
Clear the track,
tear aside the languorous shades,
the long cobwebs
that kill the way.
He who must sing
must cross all this.

The lusts and self-
indulgences you are
do not incite him much
and he need not pursue,
sees only darkness where
you howl and thrive:
dissolve, and let him through!

He is strumming a lament
for you, is ready to live
in ceaseless strain
to reach perfection in
his art, also your song—
but can do so only in
the neighboring world
where you do not belong!

Wind to Human Voice

Remember, my elusiveness
remains. All flows, all I
bring with me goes. Is it not
enough it stays, the touch
that tears across your face?
No you whisper *no*

To suffer that all passes
is as natural for you
as tearing past is true for me.
By your pain do I learn what I am.
But you too could learn that this,
my freedom is your own.

Your face shows torment at
each loss. Can you not also see
the endless stream I bring
of light, of shade, of air?
Can you not be content with
this unfailing interplay

of sun on summer grass,
of frost on foliage,
of lamps in chilly rooms?
Must you persist, must you
bemoan each time
when you are weary that

those days years back
when you ran from the sand
up to the terrace of
the summer house where you
were called, will not return?
Can you not remember instead

that you are here, although
the boy you were is dead?
That the light where waves
break out of sight
still glimmers in your head?
That in the waters' depth

the sheen is undisturbed,
only the surfaces are rough
and foul with glare? Can you
not find some comfort in
the changeless nature of my ways?
Not enough you whisper *not enough*

from **Fragments and Short Poems**

It Makes Me Useless

It makes me useless for days,
makes me walk about like
a new widow, a beggar in torn clothes:
uncompromising love
come upon
as if I had happened on
a saint's statue into whose
wooden hands
someone had placed
small coins. . .

An Absolute

An absolute:
never shall I see
coming toward me
the boy with wings
and perfect limbs
holding an apple
in his cupped hands

From Where?

From where from where
the little swallows' joy
when bells are tolled,
the sky is a pale rose,
the edge of the sea aglow?

From where from where
the little boy's love

when his father lifts him from the sea,
sets him on his shoulder,
lets him slide down his back
and later lies beside him in the boat
both asleep in the sun?

To. . .

I have sought you in gardens,
have seen you beneath trees, at dawn
merge with the dark between leaves.
I could not trap you, not then
on the lawn, nor when
you stepped from my sleep.

Must I look for you now
in these out-of-the-way places?
How shall I find you
in the dim red light
among bodies on beds,
their eyes turned from
my searching glance?

Oiseau Triste

They don't come for his sake
but to stare at something extraordinary,
a species exotic and rare.
Perhaps they wish secretly to possess
the flaming color of his breast, his wings,
or to be able to make others feel
as sad as they feel when he sings.

As for the bird, when he was first
put in his ample cage and people came
and stood behind the bars,
he trilled to be recognized as
nature's marvel that he was.
Huts and lakes and fields had not
responded to him with eyes

as did the faces stunned by
his throat and feathery moves.
He had never pleased like that
and sang for a while as he had
when he had lifted his wings
to fly beyond huts, beyond lakes
out of sight, into space.

But this, when now he tries, he cannot do.
And breaks into song not as at first
but sadly as if knowing this is so.
Still they come, some whistling to him.
Can they not tell the change in his eyes?
For he now stares at them—coldly,
not with hatred, not with rage—
watching them in their own cage.

Wilderness Child

1.

Nature was his bread,
water he loved.
The moon shimmered in the stream
he put his hands into to drink.
The moon fell through the trees
when he looked up.
Night was a silvery web.
His world of foliage and sky
trembled like a spider's threads
beneath his hands and legs.
All by himself, he howled,
not knowing how to be secure,
not knowing why the sky drifts past,
not knowing why.

2.

The hand of the man
was closer than the moon.
He took it and placed it on his head.
He pressed his cheek to the woman's breast.
What they meant and what he was
was in their eyes, their hands, and his.
His world in the wilderness
had passed him like a cloud—
not this. Here he has found
the touch and nearness with him
when he sleeps and wakes.

3.

He stands by the open window
and looks across the meadow
toward the dark wood. He has a bowl
of water in his hands. He weeps.
Is this the first time he is feeling sad?
He cannot speak but like
an animal cries out. For what
he lost? found? For what he never had?

The Door

Disgusted and in despair
I reached for the door
I can take to take me below.
It opened as though expecting me
pulled me across and I did not resist
as if this world of undergrowth
that I was entering
were my natural place.

I did not find darkness there.
No mossy branches dangling.
A white light like that in
a black-and-white film.
A canal, shallow and calm,
a gondola I stepped into
that rowed me backward to where
the stream had spurted forth
when I was born. I leaned back.

We passed a medieval church,
men on scaffolds repairing walls.
I looked in the water below.
Single figures lay asleep on beds.
I wondered how they could live
without air. Later I sat on
a bench, people were
drinking at tables
out of doors. My brother was

expected, and he came.
The water was no longer there
but everything that happened
happened as if all were part of

a flow connecting us with
where we had just been
and were about to be.
In this subterranean life
all was as it was meant to be.

The lovemaking I participated in
would have troubled me above.
Not here. Here I was not
cut off but was the stream
in this, the dream of our lives.
And was I any different when—
with equal ease—
I stepped through the door again?
And whose the dream that I was in?

A Defiance

The bird is in the sky
or wherever else birds are.
Unless it is before me
I will not have it in my mind.
Nothing shall flutter there
but what comes in uninvited.
What happens as I pass by—
in the park in the rain
in the dark under a tree—
shall happen in the mind as well.
The mind shall have no preference.

And memory too
shall not be invited.
Only what enters on its own—
like figures from incidents
that would rather be forgotten
but have come back nonetheless
and knock unbidden—shall enter;
only what enters on its own.

The mind shall be cast upon
the ground where I walk.
Let it be like fruit
that falls when it must.
Let it spill itself
as it does if it must.

The mind shall have no preference.
I shall carry it under my arm
like a helmet or a hat.
I shall put it on when it rains,
against destructive heat or stones.

I shall lay it beside me in the grass.
I shall forget it
when the sun has closed my eyes.

At a Traffic Intersection

(Hayward, California)

How large the theme,
endless, therefore comes back,
can never find itself entirely
in a single act or image,
can never be made final and
concrete the way a sculptor can
carry out what he intends
when looking upon his statue of
a woman risen from the depth, the sea—
his intention that
will always suggest this act—
he can say: "Now it is done,
is done at last. . ."

The theme is larger,
cannot be achieved in
a single portrayal,
comes back as water does—
waves upon the sand—
comes back even when
in a time of blight
the heart feels parched as
the earth looks for too long deprived of
the water that had left in it deep crags,
and there is then that despair
that what had enveloped one
as spray that flows down upon
the statue risen from the depth, the sea,
will never freshen one again. . .

But does come back when
at a traffic intersection—

130

cars going in one direction
stopped to let others
headed the opposite way
pass—there stands a stranger,
young, lightly clad, nothing in his hands,
who looks as though come from
a direction none of the cars will take,
looks ready to leap into
a distance he cannot see,
into an act he cannot name. . .

Looks ready for it there
at the intersection
waiting for the cars to pass,
waiting to give up
hoping and ready to give
what he can never give enough. . .

And while standing there
seems for many who pass him
there for them to take him away with them

back into their minds

to rekindle for some
images that have vanished,
responses they had known when
still young enough to believe
that all they had yearned for
would be achieved in

a single act of daring,
would be fulfilled by
the one single person
whose eyes become one's own,
whose arms enfold one always.

And he, who disappears from sight,
from the rearview mirror
once the lights have changed,
he, the figure that seems
to have stepped from nowhere—
from the depth, the sea, the brown
hills that fall across the valley—
he, ready, waiting, on his way:
he is the theme—
endless and returning.

Approaching a Bridge in Northern California

On the approach to the bridge
that will take me across the bay,
driving past mudflats—
seagulls, some sitting there,
others flying up and away—
I am reminded of seascapes,
of men digging for shellfish
as I've actually seen them
or remember from paintings,
and feel as I watch a gull
disappear, a plane coming in,
I am tasting the languor
of space and of time.

I'm headed for the airport.
Human habitation on the side of
the bay I'm leaving has been scant
and what there is, is recent.
Houses are all nearly the same,
much of the land beyond
has never been lived on, or worked.
And I wonder as I get to
the span that crosses the sea
what happens to the dreams of people
in houses not lived in for long?

Are dreams also empty
when the world lived in
is empty, the perspective flat?
Are they filled with
the terror that lurks in recesses
when in place of the faces that
return lost loves and lost cities
there is nothing, nothing?

Across the bridge
on the road going North
I see to my right
in the thinning fog
an enormous spacebird
setting down on the ground.

The Link

1.

Picture Ariadne outside the labyrinth
at its exit in the sunlight
bright as sand
throwing a blossom-strung thread
white streamer
into its depth
to light up
the beloved's path. . .

2.

Can you think of a more courageous act
than to face backward
and cast the best you have
best you can give
into a depth
you cannot be sure of
toward a source
you cannot see?

Cul-de-Sac

Here in the public garden
among others lingering—
lingering musically in the dark of
trees, the statues' thoughtful poses—
here in the once royal park
as you look toward the daylight
dense and dying beyond the streets

you are tempted. To wipe from you
this life that is insufficient.
To turn. To have but one
concern: the music

to be taken back
as though by someone's hand
who knows exactly where you want to reach

to return
to the gravel path's end
(or is it the beginning?)
where the park's great
wrought iron gates open
to the deep glow
of the dying light
to the music's source
the shadowed classic lawn
to your own dark shape
coming close.

To Emily

When I found myself faced directly,
eyes searching out mine
as if for fresh sightings or contest,
I thought of you, Emily
at the top of your stairs
all in white, a white branch
of greeting in your hand,
thought of you and understood
why you could not take
that first step down,
understood, when I looked into
the eyes before me,
at lips so eloquent,
how you were torn,
why you would have preferred
to turn and not descend to
the dark figure awaited
and pacing below.

Abundance, Now

1.

Out, I seek nothing
knowing that no sudden wind
no sudden apparition in
the empty street

will bring a classic hill-land back
temples atop steep slopes
philosophers and their
young disciples in a market place,
amid crafted marble in a bath.

2.

Abundance, now, must go unclaimed
must wear itself out
like any storm, must wander about
unknown, unseen, at best
a memory of bright exchange
as when one light lights up another

for those who reached out and
—startled—held, beheld: for them
at most a memory to ponder.

Two-Sided

What I love the most
is not attached,
a cloudlike shape
I think of as wandering
across some sea,
a wind-and-light fabric
between a watery surface and
low branches of a tree,
someone's whistling
so far out in the dark
you can just make out
the shadow leaping
dangerously
on the far edge of a dock.

Yet here is a paradox:
without contact made
and more than that
without at least
modest attachment
what I love the most—
the stir in the thing
that moves with grace,
fiercely independent—
does not leap in the dark
does not go whistling
in and out of sight
unpredictably
on precipitous ledges of the night.

The Rescue

We must have known each other
in a time, a life we cannot remember,
struggling from going under,
to discern the sun in a murderous storm,
must have formed a closeness then

no matter what the precise
circumstance when
struggling to rescue the body
the body within the body
that cries out to be salvaged
to be lifted from the rage of mists
into shadowed spaces of the sun.

Some such engagement must have been
ours, ours together
or I would not have felt drawn
to try to rescue with you now
that part in each of us
always in need of rescue.

As I cannot recall we had met
we must have been together then,
then or even before the time
before the crash no one remembers.

The Kiss

Now, afterward,
after the affection that rose from us both
had held us as if it too were a physical body,

now it is not the man in me
that has stepped out
strengthened into
the space the embrace has cleared
the shine of heaven

not the man, nor the youth in me
that has stepped forth like
a statue with muscular legs
into the admiring circle of crowds
that have come from far

not that, nor the girl in me
drawn forth as if summoned
and trembling behind scarves:

not these, but the child in me
unchanged and unchanging—
the child that had come out, come forth
as if lifted up
by arms out of clouds.

A Visit

You are there
remain behind at the boundary of sleep
and I can look back at you
as I am drawn away and you recede
like a white mountain from
the back of a car.

And you grow smaller, smaller
will soon be lost behind
a road, behind the actions and
appointments that make up
the hours of the day.

But you are there, there are
indications that you are
like the long, wet line in the sand,
the blossoms from catalpas on the ground,
or the smile on someone asleep

that tell of
a sea that has been there,
of a season that has passed,
of a visit
that is taking place.

The Pine

(Vence, Alpes-Maritimes)

Alone, here in this wood,
not far from town overlooking
the coast, I say to myself
I must now on my own achieve
identity with nature's things
as in the past I've had
through someone else, with
towns by the water, old streets.

Identity that I had often found
hand on hand, in arms I later
looked at lingeringly as,
asleep, they hung over
the bed's side, the windows open,
the lights on the quai and the dark ships
reflected in the harbor,
the only sounds in the room
those of the still night and of
the breathing on the bed.

Now I must on my own achieve
this union so far achieved through
another, of finding in each other
the belonging we are torn from every time,
the instant of the oneness of things,
the wave being overtaken, subsumed by
the more vehement wave,
the water both are.

                    Outside my door
there is a pine directly in
my path. Day in, day out, at night

listening to it when awake,
its stillness has been absolute.
I've put my arms around the tree,
its bark as firmly part of it
as hair on the body.

In front of it now in the doorway
a few steps away, I try to blank
my mind to really see the tree,
to let it be for me what it is,
to let it come to me. There is
a patch of sun behind, a rock at
its base on one side. A bird in
its branches twitters, twitters.

The reality of this, of the tree
and of the things around it,
flows across to me, comes to me
across the pebbly path as

quais, stonewalks, stonewalls,
a face in wateriness. . .
                              I hear
a song, a voice I cannot trace. . .

It has been held, all I now hold,
in someone else's eyes.

The Stray

(Vence, Alpes-Maritimes)

Up on the road I took each day
to walk into town, past views of
the mountains ahead, past walls
overhung with geraniums, at a crossroad
a crucifix, flowers at its base,
a chapel on one corner, a fountain across,
and always at night on the slopes
lights from homes twinkling
like stars descended: I saw one night
a German shepherd I took to be a stray
going through the garbage pails.
I had thrown out a bone I knew he
would want and I untied the plastic bag
to retrieve it; he took it and
stretched out with it on the road.
When I saw him again next night
he recognized me and, timidly, followed me.

I had been living in the woods
amid haphazard growths of wild
flowers, an abundance of broom,
pines, olive trees. I had observed
ants giving what I took to be messages to each
or greetings as they passed, had watched
tiny swallows live their shaped lives
among the branches high up in
the pines, had listened to trills
of birds I could not see, to the grinding noise
of crickets in the dense foliage;
after days, after nights
had been lulled by nature's stillness
into a stillness of my own wherein

I was beginning to discern
a common language. And to me it was

with an appeal to that shared oneness
that the dog looked at me through
the glass-door that I had closed.
No end was there to the depth in
his eyes that seemed to say to me,
that I be a steady reliance to him,
the absolute pivot in his life
was natural in the natural order
of the connectedness of things.
Indeed, he almost made me hear
the hum of this, our common flow.
The love that runs through us both,
through the wood and every creature in it
is the same. But I could not keep him.
I would be gone in a few days,
and stepped outside to tell him so.
He put his drooling mouth against
my leg. I petted him, I put my hand
upon his head; and then he left.

The Florist

In the South, in the Alpes-Maritimes,
in a resort of red-roofed residences,
cypresses, oleander in bloom, olive
trees on slopes, clipped hedges, roses,
a young man in shorts, with sturdy legs—
a local florist as I discovered since—
walked ahead of me, stopped to pet a cat
then went on and waved back to a young
woman on a balcony, probably his wife.
He could have gained something from us both,
for I felt he had responded to me also
but paid scant attention as I passed.
And he was right, of course. She will
attune him to the earth, the landscape,
the seasonal changes, to his
eventual decline. Meanwhile she
will help him in the cultivation of
his plants. And I, what could I provide?
Moments that flashed through him as he
selected flowers for a bouquet, or worked
the soil, sun-drenched and cracked?
Images of a perfection, harmony
without the discords leading up to it?
The fruit without the toil? As I am as he is,
the rare moments a culture embodies
of differences reconciled, sameness
experienced, the pleasures beyond strife
reserved for plant-life and the gods:
such moments humanized, heightened,
personalized—moments that can reach into
the essence of, the timelessness of time?
Surely he has wanted this, as he stood
before canvases, works in stone,

but stood there always in a distant way;
as when he looked long and lovingly
at light now on the roses,
light that will be there still
when their bloom is gone—
bare light, light bare as
the mountains behind this town.
To feel assurance then, the joy, relief
when the cause of sorrow, lifts, dissolves;
to experience such moments in
the most intimate, most personal
of ways, he may have missed, may miss—
but can most likely live without.
Not her—whose waiting hands are his.

The Shaper of Words on His Instruction

My response to the perfection of his limbs
—depicted often and more suitably by
painters, sculptors—came less from
personal regard and emphasis than,
I may suppose, a confluence in me
of the voiceless and a voice,
of that which gives its voicelessness,
delight at this embodiment, to words
and the word-shaper moved to praise.
For what but impersonal permanence
could view and wish to speak of this
creation of smooth flesh as a
mere aspect of the scenery
no more, no less part of it than, say,
a tree, as stable but also in
a ready pose, like a runner, set to go?
What but this supremacy could see
him motionless in motion, his elegance
unfailing and unfaltering,
and ask of the voice it instructs
to overlook, turn from the body's
vehement sexual power that however
alluring and essential to its
full beauty and male worth must end
like any other in the sod, but to sing,
sing of this human form as though
fashioned and unchanging as a god.

In Memory of Jean Garrigue

Your friend, dead also for some time,
talked of you, and there you were
miraculously before us, nothing but
spirit as you had always been
and the myriad shadowings that form
when intensest spirit and body join.
Whatever the world had added on to you
and you had had to take on for survival
as defense, with none of these, only as
you truly were stood you before us
at the mention of your name.
And when morning came and with it
waiting at my bed, day's demands that
in view of how I had just seen you,
turned to nothing but a trace
in water or air, how sharp in that
first light the boundaries were,
of the unchanging and the changed.

The Power of Art

1.

The setting is itself memory
memory's stage—
old façades and stairs
archways
to stone walks and steps
to the sea

the town's most imposing secular building's courtyard

well-proportioned arcades
windows ornamented with Gothic tracery

a portico with pillars supporting Renaissance archivolts
capitals depicting biblical or pagan themes

tall candelabra, tall candles flickering where the musicians sit

a setting of settings
as though contained in the stones,
shadows and rows of high windows
were the memory of settings—
a precise and deeply receding
perspective.

ii.
From the faces of those attending this midnight concert of songs and quartets
it is clear they're absorbed in themselves and the music.

They seem regardless of where they've come from,
regardless of childhood memories or later ones

to be taken by the music
to the same moment
the same suspension
when the forms of the setting
where they now hear the music
and the forms the setting suggests it contains,
and their memory of settings
shift and change

and they see before themselves as though through water
the musicians on chairs, the candles flickering,
the courtyard's massive shadows of stairways and balconies
and through the archways the glimmer of night on the water

see before themselves as though through water
their memories of water
of children buying apples on river barges

see before themselves as though through water
faces they have loved
the terror and the pity in the faces they have loved

and are brought to the one moment
they will have to know
or have known already:
the one terror
the same and one in all.

2.

This that you observe,
are meant to observe,
you have not made

the clearing far in the distance
sky and water glittering
on the horizon

directly before you
below you
the sea clashes against the stones

and you take in both
the light in the distance
the water moody where you stand

and you have made
none of this
whose moods are yours

and you think of the leaves
as you sat at your desk
and looked out into the yard
on a rainy afternoon

looked with a
caring, lingering
look
at the leaves
yellow and wet

3.

Before the instruments reach
the moment of momentary suspension,
in the mounting tension

a flicker of clarity
a flash of calm is espied

as though passengers holding on to the railing on deck in a frightful storm
suddenly
                as the ship rolls across a heavy wave
caught sight of

the glimmer
the glitter of calm

a strip of pure glow
way out
way off
in the distance.

ii.

When the silence is reached
there comes
from out of the moonlight
and the glimmer of the sea
that glitters in the archway

                a figure
that steps into the courtyard
moves toward the center
where for a moment
the notes are suspended and
the musicians do not play

a figure like an apparition of silver
moving with absolute intent and
inevitability
across the courtyard

across the minds of
the listeners whose eyes
are turned inward

a figure
putting one clattering limb ahead of
the other, not as a man would
but as a skeleton might
encased in
silver armor and mail.

4.

During this part of the stillness
when control
when formulation
ceases

when such realities as:
the bright glimmer on the horizon,
the thrust of the tide in a cavern

enter
whether they are wanted to
or not;

during this interval
when the music pauses—
the music having arrived at, having brought
the audience to the point when

what must come, comes;
what must be, is

and the figure clattering
does the silver dance of death—

who in the audience has not looked back
and seen a beloved city disappear behind
smoke and speed

who in the audience does not remember
hands waving
and faces utterly lost behind
steamed up glass
aware that the burden of water
has come between them,
whole lifetimes wiped out
by the start of a train?

And it is not terror then
not even pain
those who've come, who've been
listening, absorbed in the music,
are gripped by,
    not fear

but recognition

a recognition that shines up toward them
from the depth

    5.

There are no leaves on the tree in the yard

rain's silver lashings have taken them all

on the brick wall across
the rain has left streaks
irregular as downhill streams

on the radio in the other room
an oboe is playing slow passages of Bach. . .

You cannot possibly be concrete about
a feeling you loved

an urge that made you go forth
sail forth, reach out
to hold

only that it is gone
what you loved
and is too abstract to name

only that these too are gone
swept away by the silver stroke
when it had to come:

hands that you reached
bodies you slept next to
paintings you stood in front of

and much more you went toward
and can name

settings
Palladian perspectives
the Canal, the Campanile
the Colonnades
the entire huge square
in the rain

   ii.

And you remember this very room
as you stand at the end of the stone-walk

near the steps that boatmen take
and local women use to wash clothes

and you remember how you'd
met whom you'd held, what you'd
heard, what you'd said

and the music, always the music

and the sea clashing below you
against the stones
and as you raise your eyes
far out in the distance the glow
the blinding clearing where
sky and sea having merged
sky and water are no more

6.

In this moment it is not the face of many
not the setting of settings that go back to the time
when this coast was sought out as a refuge
and there was nothing there then but what nature
had formed. But those who had then settled there
from further east
brought memory
brought to the land, to its stones
memories of

rooms, yards,
lawns sloping toward the sea

and as they had built their homes
and turned the soil
obeyed them without knowing

158

memories of views of
white-walled residences,
of swans in coves,
narrow boats in inlets

for they could not, nor wished
to drive from their minds
such memories

the sea sparkling below,
the silence of the street
and the annoyance of dogs. . .

It is then not the face of many,
not the setting of settings—
it is one face that is there,
at the concert at midnight,
the faces of many become one
the memories of settings gone
when it is not music they hear
but the silence the music had
brought them to

when they see—as though come from
the water that contains so much they
remember, as though drenched in
the light of the moon, in a dance
of silver—this that they will not
escape:

what appears must disappear

who can select what is retained
for who can know how long
in dreams

paths we follow, forms we make?

7.

One face
regardless of the differences
that have made
the look, the shape, the fate
of each

one face—
resilient
resistant to time—
the face that endures

the face that has recognized
has experienced deeply that

this that is
this that I am meant to observe, to live

this that I now remember:
I have not made this
have had no choice in this

infinite the calm
so distant and yet
the glow across my eyes

close, too close
the agitation of the elements—

arms struggling, cries inhuman as
a doll's thrown to the ground—
about to engulf the path
where I must stand
have come to stand so I
may see, may know: there is
almost at the end of sight
the calm, the blinding glow

The face that states this
is, as if cast in bronze, hewn
in stone,
impervious to
fire, fog, or an
attacking fleet

dreams within dreams it holds

an interior deep as
the universe

mirrors
placed in such a way
that the view of this town by the sea,
is reflected endlessly

is retained
the proportions intact
even when
to the beholder's eye
the town by the sea,
is a dot, a star

in the depth
the dark of space

8.

In that brief silence
when the figure that entered
that comes when it must
when the figure that appeared
also disappears
and the ghastliness of
dense moonlight dancing in
a circle goes:

then it is that the faces
who've come to hear
the perfection possible in art
are in fact taken there
the instant the moment is reached
that is no time at all

—the silver figure gone
the silver slashings done—

and the faces seem to say
it is then that all creation sings

when that break in time is reached—

and there glimmers in each face
as though through a crack
the glow that shines beyond change
the glow visible beyond
the stormy clouds and waves.

Dubrovnik Festival, 1969

Muse

I kept close behind
as you whistled me on.
But now across the moody plain
late in the day
I see no tracks resulting from
a horse charged and swift
as though belonging to the sky
no dust from a cone-shaped wind

a conclusion not done. . .

am I betrayed?

But no promise was made.

In Dark's Cover

(Château La Motte, St. Firmin-sur-Loire)

1.

Almost wherever I look in this tree-rimmed
wide river's valley there are reflections,
in canals, those no longer in use covered with
the foliage's bright green refuse, in others
still trafficked by coal-bearing barges black as
their cargo, or by pleasure craft trimmed
with flags, strung-up wash, open beach umbrellas.
There are as well slender streams not deep
but rushing with strength between the fields
they nourish. Cattle come there to drink,
for a long time standing in groups in the
deep shade of the trees, enormous whether they
be linden, birches, willows, chestnut, acacias;
no matter which, the darkness they form is
the same, the patches of dark in the water
where the heads of the cattle are mirrored
and where spears of light through the branches
sparkle in the shimmering surface, the same.
Then there are amidst a variety of evergreens—
like other trees here grown to great heights
due to a favored condition of water and light—
and around the stone foundations of once
great homes, still ponds, moat-like, with narrow,
by now barely passable bridges, where float
water-lilies, shiny green leaves and other
flora that flourish in still, dark water.
An occasional magpie or wild duck
fluttering up, skimming the surface in some
pursuit, disturbs the serenity, or adds a
characteristic sound to the stillness

lingering across the ponds like the mist in
the early hours of the day. The feeling around
the ponds is grotto-like, an underwater world
of varying shades of green, creepers wound around
mossy treetrunks, flutterings from often invisible doves
high in the branches like bats in the depth of domes,
chirpings, twitterings sounding from the grotto
stillness, the watery darkness. Whose trills
from where? Whose the branches? the dark, the stillness,
the blotches in the water having wiped away
distinctions, colorations, gender, species. . .

2.

I wake from a dream, drenched by the dark's immense
cover wherein, waterlike, appearances, events
are altered, the sameness behind a striving,
an urging toward unalterable essence, glimmers
like the light the water captures and transmutes
regardless of the sky's mutedness or brightness
into the soul-soothing glow of sameness, of oneness.
A murmur, a rippling ongoingness,
the presence that remains unseen, unperceived,
is not of the nature of diversity, nor of
competitiveness or conflict, has captured me.
No recognizable shapes, nor sounds; only
the dark's soothing infused without sensation.
And the wonder, deep wonder of recognition,
comprehension.
            I had understood in the dream
that there where I was it was missing;
that violence ruled in its place; that I must
escape dislocation, must make my way back
to where the visage rests, where welcome
remains unchanged. In the fear-ridden street

someone I knew approached me and as though
he had read my thoughts, said: "We are not
separated there. Only here, where going one's own way
is assumed to be the only good, only here
are we enmeshed in turmoil, separateness."
And putting his arm around my shoulder
made me feel that I was once again embraced
as perhaps I had only been in someone's heart.
And thus flowed we on into the dream's immense
cover, the watery darkness covering sightless
indivisible light. I wake. Outside, the great
dark trees stand silent, ancient, unmoved
as time. Of their reflections in the stream
that enters the wide river down below not far
from where I've slept, their trunks, branches,
leaves, lacelike blossoms on the frailest stems;
—of all that makes them trees, nor of the sky,
dark sky between the leaves, nothing can be
discerned in the water—as though the dark,
abolishing distinctions, had blinded it.

1983

The Threshold or, My Home in Winter

1.

How often, as the years like this snow first melting then
accumulating, have drifted past, have I not had
in dreams knowledge of belonging—being back in
some scene of childhood, a tree-lined, bench-lined
city street, a farmyard, country house and garden,
when the things that rose to intimate awareness
made for what was later, longingly, thought of as
the element of home? Some assent-giving Invisible,
almost tangible evidence of the Intangible Near!
Like music that makes real our feelings,
dreams, our lives' storybook aspects, those that
are forecasters of possible fulfillments,
have often made real the reality of home
where a woman you had almost forgotten awaits you,
apparition of feelings, of music, of welcome
mysteriousness waiting on the doorstep to take you
into the secret that lives with her inside.

Yet is this house, the first I can call my own,
this house and garden where I may now belong
to what belongs to me, is this small town,
this continent where grew the music coming to me just now
from another room, on an unaccompanied cello
consolations that are the result of faith and
technique, which, combined can speak for this human need—
fulfillments so natural, so simple,
the arrival at and giving ourselves to
the one imperative none escapes,
the only thing truly familiar—is this, now
my house, my home in winter anything other than
what has always been looked toward, steered toward:
the permanent, the blissful Intangible?

For the spaces, the spaces themselves are lonely,
the mortar, new walls, old beams that support the roof
where once a ladder led, wine-barrels and bales were kept,
and the lives lived there have paled more than
the snow melting off the roof down the stone walls.
And lonely, more than lonely, cold, inhuman,
aloof when left to themselves, when not visited
by women bending to pull weeds or lay flowers,
the crosses and headstones in the snow-coated
cemetery above. An isolated sparrow sits on a wire,
sudden showers of snow are shaken from the evergreen's
dark branches. There is no one coming up the stairs,
though I had turned with a start, thinking someone
was standing there, some memory, some former presence
tongueless, amazed and staring at the changes.

And empty, empty and lonely the spaces outside.
Like a white ocean, the fields under thick snow
stretching toward the horizon and an unambiguous sky
heavy with itself, with thick moisture about to fall.
Two blackbirds screech above the moonlike whiteness.
Across the road, nothing but greyness, wisps of smoke
rising from the low houses scattered among the buried fields.
The tangible things, tangible implements
dispersed, forgotten, lonely . . .
                              A black carriage-frame
on high, thin-rimmed wheels, a decoration now
on someone's lawn, brings to mind flights
across similar scenes, trudgings that left
but flimsy tracks, of peasants driven on
by dire want, of troops of actors dragging
their sceneries, the wigged and powdered women
thrust about in the drafty wagons, the men pushing,
uttering lines long since faded on crumpled pages.

Quests, the crossings of desolate winter spaces,
the flights to known or unknown destinations,
a swarm of birds across a sky threatening, vast and
unremitting. . . grey, grey the world outside. . .
the ruts from wheels, footprints of pushing,
muttering men and boys, all by drifts absolved,
wiped out.

       And the snow-covered city streets,
the skating rink in a park an empress had owned,
a boy's attempts and failures on the ice,
the warm moments inside around a glowing stove,
the smell of wetness and burning coals,
the walk home through the bitter cold:
what of the scenery now, the foyer still frigid
but beyond the tall doors, the warm rooms,
that had described a boy's world in winter?

And of the many other occurrences we remember,
things touched, faces held, what has continued but
the sense, or want, they contained and conveyed, of belonging. . . ?
The moments of reflection, not of features
but of what we extract from them, from the forms,
from the occasion and from those who make up
the occasion, and the place and the season:
extract what is contained in them and is
the same in each, which is what we retain—
remembering the moment of remembrance
in a mirror above a mantle, in an inn
on a winter visit in a New England town.

       2.

Streaks in the sky, tracks across roads, flights
of the needy,—and who among us is not so

in this illusory world, the stations blurred,
the things attained, inadequate, discarded?
Driven by inherent impoverishment
but also by a sumptuous reality that,
though dimly perceived, has affected each
by hints in words they have now at heart,
in dreams whose unlikely musical events
surround us like silent companions,
actors have moved their sceneries, men
their households on wagons, have had to stop
and shield their eyes when the distances ahead
are suddenly consumed in a winter glare
and all that is far but visible has burst into
invisibleness. They dare not go forward, they cannot
go back. Can they take the only turn they must make
to find themselves where they have craved
to be? Shrouded in luminous nearness
the home that awaits them.

                           What prevents us
from remaining where, with unbounded tolerance,
her fullness of being that appears to us as
patience, she waits on the threshold at our arrival?

As such this grey world cannot content us on
a winter day. How often have I not listened for
the call of desiring objects, seeking forgetfulness
in bodies, the broader ranges and heightened awareness
only the contact with nearness can give?
The musical descriptions of intimacy with
the sublime! Even now, in this setting,
the possibilities haunt me, if mostly again
in dreams. Bodies together in a glow of sanctity,
luminous oneness in the guise of brother
to brother. But in this actual world

what we take away with us is solacing sorrow.
The scenes we went out to, heeding a common call,
were full with desire, the long steps in sunshine,
the flowery grasses, a solitary figure
looking out on the sea, elbow resting on the wall.
The solace we feel, having taken away with us
the sorrow of their bereavement—for we had asked
of them, had bled them for what they cannot give—
is akin to consolation in music.

                                    We are not
at home in things, only in the element of home
giving things their home.

                               Therefore is she
who would let us reside in the secret whose allure
we have longed for, even prayed for
in this seasonal habitat, now the drowse of winter,
she whose bodily opulence and cheer are but
the speech of mysteriousness to which she
would bring us, the utter expansiveness
where are dimly perceived the planes and angles,
shaped harmony of the most solid of structures
soaring and intimate, we have travelled far
to enter, the condition akin to oblivion
we come to when our desires are merged with
desiring objects—body to body, and ahead
through the open doors, the flowery grass
and the pale-colored ocean—
                                   therefore, as we come
to her, as she takes us inward, is she as well
sign of our renewed departure. For in arriving
we must also, we must still depart. "You go
to come back" I've heard it said from out of the depth,
from Him who is, above all, Immutable Steadiness.

As they alter and fade, as the things of
this world turn vague, stand as though in dreams
at the edge of nothingness, where but in us
is their sorrow, where but in us their home?
Perhaps in death we abandon them, except
that even then some spectre may linger
which a creature with intenser sense may detect
with a screech, long stare, shudder of wings. . .

The long view we have from the bridge of the river,
the surface chopped now as though covered with scales,
the vague smokiness of the winter air, the brownness
of sticks on the ground that once were twigs on trees,
the sky dark and swift:—who will lift this into
the felt sadness it pleads for, to be shared
as one shares closeness with an animal in one's arms?
how, without us, can it be winter's coziness?

O threshold, O blissful Intangible,
O concept contained in the pillar, the lintel,
music whose consolation we have at heart always:
this time-held, this wintry scene waits for us also.

The precinct that is our home is outside
of time, dimly we perceive the boundaries.
Here, vanishing things hold us, their sorrow
and the solace that comes from the moments,
the songs outside of time that return us to time,
to the wintry season where we trudge onward,
where we also belong, weary but grateful.

For it is here we rise from dreams of
her homeland, from a return of a brother
to timeless youth, to limbs resonant with spirit.
Here where I wake to the house I've dreamed of

as home, to the trees, tall, bare, not resisting
the winds; to slow wisps of smoke from the house
beyond mine; to the wintry sky in the window,
a sky grey, grim, light-streaked, and unambiguous.

The Poem of Heaven Within

to the memory of Jacqueline Rozendaal Harvey

1.

Even if now daily occurrences occasion little
to startle that part of the being that lies
in wait always, that can be roused only
by indications from that other realm
of which he, that inner part, is secret
citizen; even if now out in the streets
little happens to rouse him, as once it did,
and often—between skyscrapers, a brilliant
wintry sky reflected in walls of glass, in beams
of steel, a single gull fluttering above the street
as though it had lost its way; a clarity of
unbroken harmony, a glow of choral quality
spread over the extreme metropolis;
or, in foreign places, unexpected glimpses
of a most familiar intimacy, of a way of
being as one once knew but has not forgotten,
come to life again, suddenly, quickly,
by a garden wall, sunstreaked, silent,
only the hum of silence, blossoms, all shades
of flowers tumbling across, a path to
the house, a shape of roof, the appearance
of something contained and total
one dreams of as having remembered in a dream;
and most engaging of all, most gripping of all
the promise of love in a face not seen
until then but known and remembered always.
Even if sudden appearances of heaven's
hidden life on earth, instants of
illumination, of essence breaking through
the forms that contain it, of shudders

when observing recognition in others,
when someone is astounded by having touched
or been touched by the thing we know best,
for which there is no name but each knows
and shares, when someone is overcome by
emblems from the realm of perfection,
assurances, greetings in the way one was
looked at, or in the way the sky looked,
an opulence of clouds across an immense
landscape of tended fields and hills;
or when one is oneself startled by
the actual promise of achievable desires
others propose in their perfectly harmonious
physical presence, the containment
of the sublime in their physical forms—
observers brought to the condition of
serene oblivion by perfection that
for the least instant consumes the observed—:
even if these have lost the power
to rouse heaven's aspect in the self,
even if in daily lives such occurrences
are rare, such appearances by now
worn out, they are not so in dreams,
not when the part that is hidden there
dominates and demonstrates his truth.

2.

Is it a dream or is it actually occurring
when a most welcome event takes place?
You are on a stage, the notes you are
about to sing, words about to form
are fully shaped in you even before
you utter them, possessed as you are
by then by the bliss they mean to convey,

and as you look out into the hall,
at the faces you're about to astonish,
as you are about to start, you wake.
When the miraculous moment which you
and all those come there to hear
have already known, is about to happen,
and the corpse you are looking at
changes in its coffin before you
into the very essence of knowledge,
the very proof of the bliss you
have always been convinced exists
and is now there in the face in front of you—
o miraculous, o most welcome event!
Is the unfolding in a dream of
the one possession that remains with you
even if everything is taken away,
the secret that is left shining
like the white rose you've put before
the face that is now a photograph in your room,
the flower at the height of its flowering:
is the unfolding in a dream of that
which is secret but known any less real
than occurrences you say are real
because you are awake, but do not
remember them, those that take you
from here to there, from one
thing to another, and that is all?

3.

And of those you do remember, events
you do not want to forget, indications
of the harmonious reality that you
have always sought in encounters—
a slow drive in the country above

the wide river's ample valley,
the evening mists lifting in the fields,
the serenity when nature readies itself
for sleep; or again, the face that stands out
in a crowd, a solitary figure waiting
in a setting that suggests nothing but
anticipation—: of those scenes, cherished
events that you remember, is it not
as though they happened in a dream?
For they are always most welcome, always events
that astonish us because they are foreknown.
And when they occur, occur as though
this event of our remembrance happened there
where time's flavor is altered,
where change, the changes have shed
their shadings, perturbations, demarcations.
Birdsounds, the long light of evening,
low-roofed farmhouses scattered among
the fields, a cyclist coming out of the bushes
pedalling swiftly away on the empty road,
vast, vast the sky, the clouds enormous. . .

4.

They are not different then, for they
are, dreamed or not, indications of
an ease, a splendor completely achieved,
colors at the height of clarity,
contours of grace and gracefulness,
combined all in a simple stateliness,
simple because natural; call it
a sphere, an elevation, whose calm, order,
arrangements of parks and avenues is unaffected
by the condition you are in, asleep or not,
this source of the imagination,

this stable dominion whereof we feed.
And why but for that have you directed
yourself from early on, from when you
set forth on your dream of youth, heeding nothing but
its cause, and you sought, have sought
them always, the shades of permanence,
the long stone passages whose light, dim,
almost dull, is never altered; have sought
them in the briefest episodes,
fleetingest moments when you glimpsed
bright flowers after the rain, or sat,
forehead to forehead, arms around arms, on the bed.
Why but for that have you sought your complement,
the image you had to discern, and when
you did, felt afterward that the identity,
the intimacy was such that it had to have been
the reflection of yourself you had uncovered,
had come close to in this exploring,
this step by step accession and removal
like a boatman who loses the distance he
has gained, the shoreline at last before him:
—events in which, glimpsing the outlines of
your deepest knowledge, you lost
yourself, gaining your loss—events
which, dreamed or not, you remember.

5.

And do not call it a dream when he appears
in whom lives nothing but the splendor of
reduction, the awareness no longer perceptible
when everything that comes up before one
has been removed and what is left is the
pure bliss of irreducible being
which issues from him and touches you,

lifts up in you what has lain there dormant
and is the same as what he is only not
awakened until he appears and he tells you
that he has lived with you always,
down the corridor like the lodger of whom
one does not take much notice but who
has come now, and only he knows why now,
to at last declare you to yourself.
And you announce to someone else
who also lives with you, that he has come
at last. And you stand, both of you,
bathed in his bliss, and there is not,
there never has been any other happiness,
for this is the source of whatever it is
that has made you happy. And it is as though
even your flesh dissolved in the water of
this bliss, that even your body has become
insubstantial, nothing but the flow,
this heaven that flows nowhere, that is less
than aqueous, a shine less of a discernible glow
than of the lamps on a bridge in the darkness
below. And in the dream you can hardly believe
that this has in fact happened to you
but know it has, for you have always
known him, but inadequately; and now,
he has come before you, has declared you,
and has removed, for now, this in-
sufficiency. And the day that follows,
the day itself seems washed in the bliss
he had awakened, washed in a clarity
as you have rarely seen, as you sit
on your terrace still dazed by the wonder,
feeling no less afloat than the wind
that sways the poplars in the distance,
the lilies, strung vines and roses nearby,

touches them as though the wind itself
were nothing but a wind of light,
and the brightness is marked by a sharpness,
the darkness of shadows, of clouds, of trees,
of houses, as distinctly dark as
the brightness is bright. And it stays with you,
the effect of the wondrous encounter,
and you know it was not a dream
but the stare of reality itself
that had come to you in dream's guise.

6.

There have been times, there have been places
of a commingling, the stamping upon earth
of contours of the range beyond the range
of time, in obscurest terms
suggestions of a colossal magnificence—
man's burden, his awesome terror—
where the imagination starts,
and there walked, has always walked
one who knew, whose radiance seeped
into the soil for sustenance
and later into works composed
to encase utterances and deeds—
for we, too, are not sustained
unless joined to that of which we are—
whose plain goodwill had spread
like waters of a flood into the sleep
of all. And the voices you hear today,
always high as though in imitation of
the child, or aspiring to reach,
with trumpets as support, the end,
the limit of sound, are at once
from lofty spaces and residual chambers

you have within yourself. And when
you can, you prefer to go for this accord
to where the hymns, modulated as
in supplication by a humble bass,
were sung, and even if the squares
are silent and you hear the water splash
against the stones, the strong sun
casting long and lingering shadows on
the walls, there reverberates each time
within yourself a response to what once
was there, imprints still of what
not time nor denials could erase.

7.

What are your thoughts when on waking
the heavenly voices are vanished,
or you are back to the untrodden spaces
arid like stellar surfaces where you
have lived for long and you are met
again by faceless hooded shapes that
creep in as soon as heaven's troops
are gone, or where they have not yet been?
—those shades of drabness, lingering traces
of early agonies that also live in you
but in perennial webs of mist,
the hurts that claim their origin
far back in the ancestral birth. . .
"Reclaim, react, rebel, defy! flesh that
you are and you need not, cannot defy!"
Like snails to moss on walls, clinging
to loss, dissatisfactions, lead you
to heightened fantasies, acts that
do not abolish, as they suggest,
but only strengthen them, who claim

and have this hold on you by this,
that you are human because of them.
Any reprieve into the glare
of heaven's light where they
must fall apart like ash, enrages them
—like wasps that strike though they
must die—to monstrous irritations.

8.

It is not they who make me what I am,
those hordes freed all around me, freed since
the images that had controlled them fell
and people turning from their hold on them
made room for grievances long hidden and
denied, the darknesses in them too long
ignored, the hurts too long repressed.
Now they occupy the sad terrain strewn with
the broken imagery, pieces of noble heads,
rumps of horses misshapen into the dial
of time, the rummage of idols and of dreams
the sole possessors of the sunset scene.
A death announced but not an heir. They are
the furies who, once freed, release themselves
in each. As they have done in me,
who, for a while rebellious at a
rebellious age, took up their cause.
But recognized them as the source of
misery and, struggling for distance, broke
their hold on me. For it is the destructive force
they serve, discontinuity, ego-
centricity, the never ceasing demands
of the disgruntled self, prodigal, expelled.
Once seen for what they are, they change
their guise, proclaim themselves on heaven's

182

side, that it is they, the acts they indicate
which are our means toward it, though all
the while, insidiously, feeding the doubt
—which sense proves it?—that it exists.
Chameleon-like, lecherous for nothing
but to survive, arch-enemy of man,
it is not they who make me what I am.

9.

But what they oppose, that stands fixed,
compassionless in their regard,
opposing them, has made me what I am
far back as I recall. In earliest sights
of luminous distances,
of hills and waters, slopes of vine,
of ample lawns and darknesses of trees
in parks full of a lingering pomp
of time, of silences, of broken or-
naments, of stone; in faces, later on,
a comprehension caught in eyes
of loss, of hopes, of possibilities—
young intimations of
supreme acknowledgment
expressed as love, and of its pain;
for nothing lasts in this our human realm,
the eyes, the slender hands confessed.
And mostly, that I looked even then
before I knew what suffering was
upon a suffering face with pity—
for a mother's inability to change
the course of things, reverse a fate,
or as a boy for a friend whose boyish limbs
as he stood, arms crossed, near where
I sat, spoke to me first of

the fragility of our lives.
From where, that early on, the need
to give assurance, and of what?
To say to someone struggling with
a loss, divesting himself as though
digging frantically, of the life
that has kept him apart, the outerwear,
the piles of paper he doesn't want,
to be close again to the secret intact,
the substance, the salve of the gods:
that it is there, from where we've come,
that all along it has been undisturbed,
that it cannot be reached as place,
which never disappears as it does not
appear, there where our home resides,
the gleam we here perceive belongs,
the unseen throbbing like air following
a burst of bells. . .

10.

They come, also in dreams, the mistakes
of every age, wander about in the vast
mist–held fields of their regret, figures
whose minds are gone, who cannot weep,
who come to us that we may weep for them,
so they may fade, by retracing far as
we can, by digging out from our memory
the cause that caused the error to begin—
o error, error that must plague us
the more that heaven's shine, some com-
prehension of the origin brings into view
the mists wherein they must remain encased,
the torments that may fade but never quite
dissolve, o disconsolate figures

that are to us what misshapen forms
must be to those who brought them forth,
whom they must pity if not love,
or love the more for their complicity
in the emergence of distorted lives.
Nor is it just in dreams where this
disturbance lies. The causes of
disharmony being so many and so old,
to be rid of the great roar of their demand,
the power in the blood, have we
not done, have I not done, as they
would have us do? But the great, the patient source
in us is merciful. It is not asked
that we do any more than we can do.
It is not asked that we be killed by their
attack. Only that we do not favor them.
That we battle, but not be on their side.

11.

There will be moments, and they have already been,
you may be aware that they have,
or that they eluded you
as the brightness of certainty,
as knowledge does when we wake,
the times when the person you are,
the desires that have both shaped and unsettled you,
longings and errors borne by the very stones,
the very fabric of the setting
into which you came, walks, rooms,
tall squares dark as sleep,
amongst which you have moved and move,
also at the end of passages
sudden views of spaces bright as sun,
an ocean before you or a descent

of valleys, flowers, flowers,
field after golden field turning into distance
and a blue arising, unearthly, ethereal. . .

There will be moments
when all that the past has made you,
that is present within you,
has sunk to the ground, lying there
passive, humble like initiates
their foreheads touching the floor
deferring to a greater force, the greater force;
or, like a master's hounds sitting,
their paws stretched before them,
seemingly listening to the master speaking on his return. . .

There will be moments
when you are not there,
when your terrors, hopes, even your secrets
lie obedient as though non–existent,
and there takes hold of you
the greater force that also exists in you,
and it takes hold of you
like the dance of the dancer,
the creator of what he has created

and as you lift up your leg
in the dance of his dance,
as you lift up your arm
in the reach of his hold,
as you hold up your head
in the pose of his might
and as there falls from your eyes
the joy of his joy

there is then nothing but

the shimmer of his shimmering being,
his shimmering vastness and
the shimmering sounds,
the trembling sounds of his joy. . .

and the earth is his shimmer,
the fields, the trees and the stones,
and the water and the sky
his shimmering flow that
has never never been
anything else, never anything
but what it is. . .

and you let it happen, it has become
itself in you, and you do not
hold on to it, you let it be,
you must let it be, you do not try
to have it happen again,
you did not bring it about

you only let it be
you let it be
that which was you
that which is you
and is gone

12.

There is only this that you must do
if the cry in the depth of your being
heard by you in the best of dreams,
by others seen in the far-away look
like the language of yearning in your eyes;
if—other gratifications not withstanding,
acts of the body the body demands,

forgetfulness and the reach into
the taste of the timeless, the place, limbs of
the gods, the body can accomplish—
if your deepest, your relentless desire
is for unceasing closeness to
the precincts, even the outermost stretches,
watery borders, lights reflected and swaying
as in lagoons around the canal-crossed city;
if what you want ultimately is to be near always
to at least the furthermost reaches of heaven.
There are, on earth, places, not only fortresses, cities
but coasts blue as bright midnight, inlets, coves,
blending the gentle aspects of water and land,
of colors, of homes, of gardens, and there
are fields and there are streets and squares
and tree-bordered lawns and ponds which suit
the hidden aspect, the grandiose but gentle concept
that is the hidden world of heaven,
are appropriate to, approximate its nature,
are the visible expression of its invisibleness.
There have been men and women, men and women
who when immersed entirely in heaven within,
when absorbed by it, looked upon their earth,
cancelling thereby the demarcations, making
of what is within without, and without within;
their look, that look cast then, the instant of
this merging upon earth—having thus
transformed the land, its essence expressed,
heaven's contours brought forth—lasts still.
So you must try to stand. In harmonious
relation to the invisible in you
which only your reception of the given world,
your acts, gestures, looks, words can
make visible. And do not ask that it
possess you, that it break through in you,

becoming itself in you, as once,
or perhaps more than once, it did.

13.

A drive to Pontlevoy, past fields
of heather, of corn, past sunflowers tall
as wheat, each in the vast field turned
as in one huge obedience toward the sun.
How many drives have there not been,
at midday, or sunset when
the flowers have turned the other way,
to visit friends, meet trains, or just see
the countryside, walk through towns.
How many places have we not seen
that are nowhere now but in reflections,
like the entire ascending side of a town on a hill
in the wide river we drove along
on our way back in the evening, all that had seemed
solid, the trees, lampposts, old walls,
nothing but the watery flow
we possess in the end. The sixteenth-century
abbey, the Sun-king's symbol in stone
above the door where the Dauphin had slept—
added impressions in a stream of
impressions, of pomp
once real, of façades once decorated
for arrival or a death. Only
the look, and no matter how many, there is
only one, only the look that receives,
has received that which is actual,
only that look remains at the end of day.
Appearances, not as fixed and solid
but as flowing, as reflected in
the wateriness of time, as contained

forever in the river that flows
nowhere, that is the view of heaven.

14.

For us, nonetheless, irrevocable departures,
always the loss. And of that other denial
far more wounding than the illusion of
appearances, than the betrayal of time. . .
That it cannot be had on earth,
too many examples are told of it,
the beloved beyond human measure,
the beloved, fleeing, caught forever as a tree;
nations warring because of one man's reach
for the love beyond man's power to possess;
a youth tricked by poisons from attainment,
his desperate schemes to make permanent
what he had glimpsed, had had, of bliss,
but fleetingly; another man's rage, revenge
in murder when the love he had possessed
was ruined by another's envy and deceit:
none of it can last, can be made to be
possessed, heaven's hidden lineaments,
heaven's bliss the body has.
And for those who must reach that far,
who are not content unless they have found
in another, in a burst, an illumination,
the features they have sensed in themselves,
their most cherished, hidden visage
in the total person, pose of nothing but
perfection, in the other, in the other's arms;—
for those who are not complete, and they
have always been among us, who cannot cease
to quest for the very reach that has made them,
are not complete unless in one touch

they have touched and been touched by
what is behind each creature, uniting all:
for those who cannot cease unless they
have thus been loved, and love—how do
they live with this injunction, that henceforth,
though their desires do not die, their
demands must cease? That it must be enough,
times passing, the passing images of love!
That it cannot be made their own, cannot
be brought into their realm, that they
must let it fade from them, dissolve—
the body of perfection they have seen,
a descent of heaven standing in the river,
perfection in the body standing in the water,
in a gathering distance, a gaining haze.

15.

Invariably, having been close to the courts
that aroused the awareness of heaven in me,
of harmonies, scenes mine once and now
vibrant again, that brought them to life
again, in actualities, in dreams;—
far away places, the silhouette of him
who lifted my being up, who swept by,
a white cloth over his shoulder, almost like
a being of air, almost as though he weren't there,
leaving a trail of blue, remembrance
of love hurt, young love hurt, restored,
a bloom of deliverance in my eyes,
the child's hand in his mother's, the world
well again, innocence real once more. . .
Or walking in streets, squares, towns,
the countryside around them as artful as
the art it produced, of harmonious

perspectives, of the lady of modest demeanor;
or in dreams when I found again a brother's
love, and there exists between us a oneness
as in the looks of those bound by
the same love, the love for him in whom
it is incarnate, and it is in the dream
engaging, fulfilling, heightened, amorous,
the love in brothers for one another
and for the love that is the same in them. . .
Invariably, there follows then
a rousing of old wants stirring the body's
irritants, an urge that would lead to acts,
to scenes that can well be imagined—
the opposite of the courts of benevolence,
of the gracious bestowing of love,
the settings, details of the blood's rage
having been depicted, recounted often enough.
Invariably then, let it be said,
loss and longing for his benevolence
having made one find one's way back,
he is there on one's return, unchanged,
attentive as though awaiting one,
the fullness overflowing, overwhelming,
for who but he knows the conflict he causes
—indifferent, implacable, immovable?

16.

Since the solid, indicated world
is only seemingly so, appearances
vanishing as if dreamed, the slopes,
uphill, downhill, scenes we look at
longingly, of shady gardens, roofs,
of cattle sitting, horses drinking at ponds,
of rolling hills whose gentle aspects

caress us as we pass them giving us
the restfulness, blessed assurance
we seek, deprived of them—of a soil
so drenched—in someone's arms; since these
and other scenes we live with, have lived with,
occurrences long ago, whole ages recorded,
their achievements viewed now as ruins,
as remnants, as grand, often extravagant
displays on walls; since whole ages gone
and the years of our lives we remember,
scene after scene of the solid world
dissolve, rise up to us, live on
as our remembrance, often our torments,
secrets that have to be released or it
is killed in us, our ease with it, with this
their continuance, reception:
Since even the expressions in the body,
the realization in human form of
the stature that belongs to nothing but
permanence, immanent, invisible,
is for us always shrouded in distance,
perfection glimpsed but never owned,
heaven's look looked at that will hound us
as only beauty in the body can,
will run, all our lives, through our days:
—Since nothing that yields itself
to our perception is solid, permanent,
what of that that lures us on, that is
not caught in its appearances? Is it not
in us? Does it not hide in us
without whom appearances would not
appear, would not record, reflect
themselves, their splendor not resonate,
perfection not be recognized,
the ideal they possess, remembered?

17

He rules there, is not hidden, lives,
nearer than nearness, as though hidden,
in the depth of our being, hangs on our eyes
just as we wake, just as we look upon
his form in the first form before us,
the shape that has risen in our eyes,
space and time having become the shape
that has risen to be recognized,
that has risen to be received.

He rules there to where each returns.
Out of him, in us, the splendor we look at
on hills, the sights now wasted;
out of him, in us, the love in the eyes,
the light in quickness in the face
before us, in the hand ours moves toward;
out of him, in us, the complete body
standing before us, the sky as backdrop;
out of him, in us, the perfect body
standing at a distance in the water;
out of him, in us, the harmony
as we sit near a lamp, our eyes closed;
out of him, in us, the music
of farewell, of hopes for a safe journey,

the music we hear in the dark,
in a dark square in our sleep,
that speaks of the heart, consoles and consoles. . .
out of him, out of him
on our eyes, our depth,
the secret dissolved,
the secret cleared as we wake. . .

the years are gone, the ages
but he hangs on our eyes as we wake
and is the same

★   ★   ★

18.

For days I've been as in a blissful slumber
although the impressions of things around me
have never been more vivid, of the four poplars
taller than pillars at ancient sites, their tops swaying, rustling;
of the hill beyond, or of the massive stone supports
where the bridge starts that leads a canal across, above the river
on whose bank we walked, sometimes wading through puddles
left by the river or by yesterday's storm. Although I've been
as in a daze, the reception by an invisible flow, firm essence of
my being, firmer, no doubt, than the stone supports
or the roots permitting the giant treetrunks to sway
as in a steady rhythmic ritual, solemn dance,
—the reception of details never more vivid
has never, unless in a dream, or on occasions
so rare only the wholeness can be remembered,
the details a blur: has never, or rarely been
as unimpeded, as immediate, the impressions
seeming to become at once the air that held them
and the invisible essence, depth that received them.

And as I listened during these days to some of the great works
the composers of two, three centuries ago have left us,
and even of those more recent who struggled still
and in the end succeeded to find again and state again
a faith, a purpose, a redemption (one such work engaging
a thousand instruments and voices), I felt that it had all come together,

all that can be said, demonstrated of value, demolishing
every notion so that the one thing, one essence, only fact,
fixed fact that moves us, can be revealed, can be allowed to be itself. . .

And I thought, almost hearing it said, that the masters have said so,
it has all come together. . . the compassion, the structure
—no sound, no language, no form
giving music its sound, language its strength, form its purpose—
invisibleness giving myriad shapes, myriad constellations, form, grandeur,
                                              flow. . .

it has all come together. . . in utterance, in the look,
the caring look upon the supplicant, the caring look
upon the soil like hands lifted in blessing

it has all come together. . . at the source of utterance,
where the needy, the restless dead, the spirit neglected
in living things, gather timidly in the rose–light of evening
in the shadow of palms. . .

And I thought, the masters have said so, in music,
in intimations, in silence: it has all come together
in him, in him who has walked, invisibly, yet visible,
who is always the same, the changes equal at his eyes,
who walks and will walk, freeing at each step
the delightful being on his shoulder, giving back
to air what is air, to spirit what is spirit,
making us aware at each step, at each step making us know
the miracle, one miracle, the unknowable, unperceivable, constant and
                                              forever.

And I thought: As I am, and know that I am,
as I am sublimely awake, adrift in this blissful slumber,
why would I doubt? And I looked at the poplars,
at the wind deep in their branches,

at the evidence of wind deep in their branches,
and I looked at the bird and heard it pecking on the wire whereon it sat,
and I looked at the dove, the grey mourning dove flying off
its perch below the roof across, making its mournful sound;
and I looked at the stones of the wall where I had put my hand,
and I looked at the vines, and when I got up and walked,
at the fields, rolling fields stretching far into the distance,
and at the trees, dense trees bordering them,
and at the child running before me: and they do not doubt,
do not doubt that they are.
                              And voices came to me, chords,
voices in chorus, and from one of the masters, the most lyrical,
shattering song on the clarinet, from out of my sleep, the bliss in dreams,
the bliss awake

                    ★   ★   ★

By the water, by the wide river,
below its bank on the stones
where the river has receded,
by the water and the small islet
the river makes, stretches of sand
where the child, naked, plays,
the father stands in the water fishing
and the mother lies in a chair sunning;
by the water, seeing the family,
looking at the trees on the bank across,
at the width of the river, its changing shape,
at the islets, sandy, stony, some
with clusters of bushes, some with trees,
—looking at the river, end to end,
its forms, its borders of stones, of trees
some with roots exposed like veins of mud,
and looking up at the vastness—
above the enormous range the river makes,
the width of its bed and higher, its valley—

stretching, vaulting above all
the sky's deep blue streaked in parts
by trailing threads, or scarves, of leisurely clouds;
—by the water, by the wide river
the unencompassable height hovering there
like a being, all of it, sky and water,
width and length, child and fisherman,
and over there, a dog wagging its tail
for a stick to retrieve from the water,
all of it, all of it become like a being,
one unencompassable, unimaginable yet almost tangible
being, whose presence runs through me,
whose presence breaks through me
to thrills beyond feeling except that I know,
that I know I am moved beyond feeling
and that I am one with, encompassed by
as each thing, each living thing, each element around me
is, all of us held in the oneness of the being
that is there, is actually there, in and
beyond us, holding us, the creator, the created,
the essence hovering, I can feel it hovering,
the essence blessing, loving, enjoying what it is

(Châtillon-sur-Loire)

198

On Another Departure, Châtillon 1987

When silence enters and past times
are recollected as though a lens
had caught beloved images restored
to a brilliant sharpness they may or
may not have had when first perceived,
their look of timelessness down lanes
behind an ornate iron gate slightly ajar;
when such images of moments of former
happiness come back, of people and places,
the ease and oneness between them,
a walk, arm in arm, across a bridge;
among trees dimly lit by lamplight
the tentative urgings of desire:
the longing these arouse in us is not so much
for what actually happened as for
the promise they held, the sweet
anticipation as they occurred.
Years have had to have taught us that of our ardent wishes
little has become real; of the beloved visage,
although appearing before us, there has been
no lasting possession. Ultimately, the perfection
of which we receive glimmering impressions—
around houses, canals, faces looking up
at our approaching shadows—exists,
continues in its impenetrable realm,
its own glory of constant presence,
for us out of reach except that we
perceive, except that we may feel it. Reminded
of moments charged with its promise,
we continue to look longingly toward
the gate of forgetfulness where at last
we shall be at home, absorbed in
the quiet splendor of its wholeness.

Old Offense

It seems to me in retrospect
I held you as a charioteer
maneuvering his reins holds
the road flying past his wheels,
or as a youth cradling a fawn
lured to his moonlit lawn.
But I was neither racing toward
a shore in antiquity
nor trapping animals to appease
an adolescent's lust.
Another ancient hunger drove me
to seek you out where you, like I,
had come to find more than a
reflection in a stream,
though as capture no more solid in
the end. For, the instant that
you glimpse in someone else's
features a vision of yourself,
familiar but so far back
it does not come up before you
in a mirror, sight blurs,
the injured moment runs,
the flesh in your arms turns
from watery shimmer to stony
stare: and you let go
the damp head in your hands
as if you had transgressed,
had relived an old offense.

Spirit's Taunt

You will not see me
unless you dare storm the body,
break down frontiers and enter
where all sorts of injunctions
tell you you must not.
Forts have been put up
for more than territorial defense.
Shy the face peering out
behind a latticed window.
A box within a box within
a box within many more
holds the piercing treasure.
Behind walls deep in
the central courtyard
blooms the mysterious flower
the color of flesh.
Only from there will you
hear me, see me, will you have
the consolation that I am.
But that is all. I will
cover my face, will pierce
and blank you out if
once there you will try
to take what is not yours—
will think you may remain because
you have dared storm walls
forbidden you by laws.

Dark Converse

Like a block of ancient stone,
mausoleum slab or one that marks
the spot where the oracle sat,
a deep inexplicable darkness sits,
too habitual to be dissolved, more of
a riddle after all these years;
and when it flares up, flares up
as hurt that cannot be righted,
desire that cannot be quenched.

The dark converse this
of another indication equally
unbroken, of radiance that
on many occasions has flowed
across a face, down a body like sun
in a room on a torso of stone.

Signals

It is not a permanence they seek
(that can be permanent only for
a limited time), it is the fleeting
wherein alone the permanence
that is not limited can shine:
other-than-human beings in human form,
perfect limbs that grow out of
clouds, out of mists, then walk alongside
on dusty roads they took, angels
who impart messages, then leave.

They who seek are in the audience,
have come for nothing less than
a great event, a dancer who in a leap,
a turn can outdo the pulls that hold
others in place; or to hear a pianist
who in a chord, a phrase brings back
the look each has met at one time,
the face that time does not erase.
Or they're in a bedroom seated at
the edge of the bed, rid of

their clothes, about to embrace
the other in whom may ascend
the figure both yearn to apprehend;
about to rediscover in private,
in secret, the known, the beloved,
the quintessentially familiar—
for whom, when the signals are there,
they will have come; for whom,
for however brief a time, they will
have left their ordinary lives.

77th Street Fair

As usual, from the moment I wake
and adjust myself to where I am,
(as in a lens by adjustment
so that images appear in focus
as of a galloping rider observed
from mountain tops by marksmen
through a lens on their guns)
—as usual, as day proceeds
I am aware of absence.

Sunday. I walk down a sunny street.
A fair is going on. Stands
for food and merchandise; a caravan
of baby-carriages occupied and led
by ribboned Persian cats; a handful
of onlookers, some with fine, delicate
faces, stand around a young man playing
a Bach aria on the flute: "I am
not lost" it says, *I am not lost!*

Around the corner the crowd disbands.
There is the whine of emptiness
as of projectiles whizzing past.
I spot a figure up ahead.
Adjusting myself to this possibility—
your presence in the empty street—
I find, after all, it is not
your shape that's there, only its space,
its space like a cutout of emptiness
ablaze in windless air.

Mozartian

(On the Long Island Expressway)

I must not let it get away,
the song I dreamed I sang,
Mozartian tunes of an
assuredness only one
element that sings through us
is capable of. It surrounded me
as I had lain in the dark: return
not loss of those we loved with
our changeless selves, this un–
demanding love the song
conveyed; flickers of
its shadow on the dream's
tall squares, old stones,
stayed on into the day.

Now, under a wintry sky,
along the highway and amid
a stream of cars (on a sparse lawn
a man huddled in his coat
impatient for his dog
to stop sniffing and be done),
now as I talk to the others
and we can only reach so far
—irritations mostly—
I turn when nothing is said
to be sure that it is there,
to listen for it, to hear
far far back in the dark
its unchanged song, its unchanged lilt.

Mozart in Châtillon

From Salzburg, the quartets named
for Haydn. As always in Mozart,
the second movements touch us the most.
It is early autumn, the green still bright
in the already thinning light.
Here and there, there is a brilliant red,
soon the winds will whirl up, will wipe away
the yellow leaves along the edges of
the road that mark the sidewalk.
The cat across has placed herself
upon a pole, captivated by the sight
of butterflies; like us, she is
bewitched by what she cannot catch.
What do they reach in us, those slow,
those sombre chords? Recognitions,
regrets, finalities that in the end
we must accept? Memories, of course.
Of myself, a boy of twelve, at a concert of
the school orchestra where I sat last
among the second violins; and that,
spotting my mother in a front row,
affected by her distant beauty,
I had sensed, however vaguely, even then
her sadness, the irreversibility
of choice, the stubbornness of fate,
and could not, much as I might
have wished to, alter any of it.
Others, more glorious, but also sad,
as if, even when they occurred
they contained the pain of
the irretrievability that we
would surely one day feel. Images,
of travel, of Mediterranean skies,

of domes sparkling, of canals glittering,
gondolas crossing, of beaches, cliffs,
of gardens laid out to please,
of amorous moments under trees,
of pleasures still prospering.
How much we have loved
so much of what has left us!
And now the season that is over,
what of the calls, the visits, drives,
the stops at cafés, the views of churches,
the intimate talks, the dinners outdoors,
what, if any of each, will we recover?
Is the most that we can have of love
the knowledge that it passes?
Odd then, that at least as long as
the music lasts, we should not feel
deprived, but taking us back as well
to moments of sorrows lifted,
to solace (the genius's assurance of
a steadiness, of a love that does
not fade?), we are moved, wistful
but moved, by Mozart replenished.

1992

from **Memory Fragments**

Across the lavender fields
vast and sloping downward steeply,
below them a ring of newly built houses
and then the beach, the sea;
across the bluish fields swaying lightly like a lulling sea
the sky's color similar to the fields' though a bit deeper
more like the color of the sea as I imagined it would be
(I could glimpse it far below from where I stood),
the medieval town in back
the ramparts and the town's interior by law unchanged;
across the lavender fields
ascended from the town's central fountain
ascended from the stone rim of the basin filled and glistening,
from there ascended
to fly across the fields
the lavender fields toward the sea
and flying deep and deeper into the deeply bluish sky,
the white doves
that will no doubt return
to sit again on the filled basin's rim—
birds not of transit
but of the disappearance into permanence.

(St. Paul de Vence)

★　★　★

Once again driving above them
slowing down for the view
the fields spreading below us
made ready but not yet harvested,
the carefully tended earth giving off
a haze as though a contained vastness

as well as the visible distances
that ring the fields on all sides
where earth meets sky at its descent
had settled down and across
the crops of wheat, of corn, of sunflowers to come,
bestowing on all the peacefulness
that may break out into our dreams,
hidden designs we recognize
as we move slowly past and as
closer to us we spot a dog
stretched out across a doorstep.

(Cernoy en Berry)

★   ★   ★

It is the deep moment I am after,
that quick occurrence that escapes notice
like the instant when a wave in a tossed sea
falls from a peaked height back down into
the sea's vast turbulence, back into its watery
essence, its calm. As, for example, the time when
waiting at the port as a dear friend
steps off the gangplank, or when later
we speed across the bay to the rooms rented in a villa,
or when later still, the morning after and
the morning after, we come down for breakfast
set for us in the overgrown, now neglected garden
of a former summer residence. When that and
so many other incidents clearly of significance
or they would have escaped
the moment I seek now to recapture,
when the event dissolves into the secret it carries,
the promise of its permanence—
like the barge in the canal

that appears to have disappeared
when a thick fog has settled over the water.

(Dubrovnik)

★   ★   ★

The sky
a damaged blue like sheetmetal brutally treated,
the river
risen to almost the danger limit,
the surface mercilessly beaten,
only the sanctuary near its bank
rising straight into the sky's lowered height
remains solemn, steady, indifferent,
the bells tolling as always just when they're meant to,
the needy struggling at the regular hour
toward the awesome portal,
the nail-studded door so tiny by comparison.
It's not the winds but the dissolving voluptuous shapes
gathering above and hovering on steady wings
that continue to howl and hiss their hallelujahs,
the storm-torn fragments of their changeless songs.

(St. Benoît)

★   ★   ★

Rachmaninoff's "Symphonic Dances"

Yearning, pure and simple.
For what, where, whom
remaining abstract,
only the melody,
romantic, sad

as now the reminiscence
of having heard it long ago
in a room that opened out
into the bay, the city lights below,
thinking then as now
of so much that we desire;
as then, as I sat listening
I thought I had seen it expressed earlier that day
not as such by the young man
I had observed as I drove past him at a crossroads
but by his desire for a car to stop
and take him along into some designated distance
to someone, some entrance, some narrow path to the sea,
some patch of blue and the sun sparkling,
to at least some fragment
if not all of his desire.

(Hayward, California)

★   ★   ★

Birds trilling on, trilling on
despite the rotten weather
chanting as they always chant
despite a sky for days now
floating, grays dissolving into grays
swiftly as though in chase of
a disturbance causing disfigurement,
causing the most grievous offense,
heaven's absence and of the sun
mirrored in ponds now filled
beyond extremest limits, the nearby farms
in danger of this overflow.
A rapid fleet, the sky, in chase of
piracy, but the birds trill on,

trill on indifferently
remembering perhaps blossoms-heavy boughs,
recalling to us what cannot be obscured or lost,
a perfect sky and garden where
their chants add to a not forgotten calm
and the bees not scattered or disturbed by any storm
drink where they can, the nectar from the sun.

(Châtillon-sur-Loire)

★   ★   ★

Crossing the square
in a medieval town high atop a hill,
two boys, eight years or so,
arms around each other, held tightly,
paying no attention to what
they have lived with all their young lives,
and tourists facing the scenery
from a promenade below the ramparts
have come from far to see,
the vastness that extends all around
their town, the impervious dignity
of space blending so naturally
the clouds with the sparkling edges of
the valley where the river dissolves into
the sky: how could these boys sense
that a love greater than the expanse
that surrounds them from all sides,
now holds them,
already working its wonders through them.

(Sancerre)

★   ★   ★

The autumn fields lie in contented resignation.
Having been tended—attentively
by all, lovingly by some—
and given of themselves to the fullest,
they have achieved the satisfaction
that follows total response.
Docile, peaceful,
their colors, though vivid still,
not those of former anticipation,
of golden pride,
but reduced now and sombre,
here and there spotted with
a deep red leaf
from fading trees and bushes:
just ahead of the long rest to come,
in this moment of fulfillment
lifted into the realms of art,
display its harmony.
And we, passing by,
respond to this achievement
as though something in us
recognized in it
and in the promise ahead
our own destiny and desire.
Under a sky of heavy clouds,
most grey, all dark, some black,
a blackbird crosses the long distance.

(Barlieu en Berry)

Two Swans at Ousson

On my way back from a walk
I frequently take along the Loire
here where the river is especially wide,
where there are always men and sometimes boys
fishing from the bank
or standing in the water,
and where much further out
colorful rowboats often come by
and along the opposite side
on what must be sandbars
terns sit or stand,
I noticed a pair of swans.
As always I was startled by
their beauty, by their grace
but then, as I stopped to observe them,
by the precision, one-pointed
attentiveness with which they
pursued their aim, which was
to find their food.
     To be clear
about one's need and be focussed
on nothing but it! To have nothing but that
as one's target!
     How I have swayed
from mine, as always on my walk,
when the calm, the shady path, the water's
gleam lead to thoughts
of what the years have brought
and of what not, and of how
to satisfy renewed demands
for fulfillments that—
as I have had by now
sufficient occasions to recognize—

not the body but only that in us
which asks for nothing can provide.

Such the contents of scenes flashing by,
of encounters with landscapes that pass,
of meetings that met a flared-up need,
of the substance inward and serene—
as then the water's surface at my side—
from where desires feed
and hence to where and not
entanglements too often tried,
the craving points.

            Watching the swans,
the movements of this elegance,
watching them apply the refinement
that nature can achieve when in pursuit of
what each must live on to survive,
watching them focussed on that need
as, not diverted by the slickness of
the slender rowboats racing past,
nor by the seabirds squeaking from their corner,
they thrust those most graceful of necks
in a sudden stab to where they had perceived
swam or hung the object of their need
and as, rising, resume their incomparable poise:
I wished for a one-pointedness like theirs,
to at last direct desirous thoughts only
to there, to deep within, from where alone—
as did the swans in their contented glide—
I may rise fulfilled and satisfied.

Magician

1.

Out of dim reaches he rises,
his features indistinct, a blur aglow
in a distance indeterminable in
vapors that lift and lift as though
from marshes, his features indistinct,
his presence unmistakable.
Time and history, the figures
of greatness he inspired, whose names
remembered, whose works are forever his,
are in back, are ahead of him
in the prevailing mist. A head
lost in rivers, the books others flung
into flames, the songs still issue from him
whose shape is indiscernible,
whose message has outlived all who once
were his. Where do you come from?
I've often wondered and wished to ask
feeling him near. I see no halls on mountains
inaccessible to man, no city brilliantly lit,
no anointed golden youth on his knees
before a throne strumming sweet songs.

2.

Nearing, he points some sort of staff
that is like a blade sheathed yet effective as
a foil, aimed I feel to where the heart is.
A weapon fierce and glistening as though
lightning cracked from it, pointed at both,
the harmonies and behind them
the discordances which, what but the heart

must overcome—before reaching the fields
where spirits promenade and sing—
the deep, dank darknesses where those
of unrelenting griefs, those whose lives
were unfulfilled, now hide
in clustering groups and wail.

3.

O sorely tried, that it must come to this,
to have to face torments, endure miseries
dissolving from their hiding place
as lamentations, as winged blind creatures might
from cracks in rocks to which they've clung
until the thinnest shaft of light
penetrated to this, their desolation, their despair;
joy's opposite, now by his pointed thrust,
an inescapable command, released.
O sorely tried, to endure extremities,
whether in utter silence in cloistered cells,
or in descriptive—rich in colors, rich
in floating garments—domes,
the sufferings of discontents
wailing upward for redemption, for relief:
to endure this struggle toward the source,
there to dissolve into the background where
he, where you alone reside and rise—
to endure the urgent plea of each
to come back home, back home to peace.

4.

Out of dim reaches he rises,
has risen into faces, up into eyes
that have visualized him

in melodies that conveyed to them
features they could not define but knew
hearing them musically expressed,
or when in the face, the eyes of others
they passed, they recognized them
in their pensiveness whether they
were directed toward something
gleaming far out in the distance,
beyond fields, perhaps no more than
a strip of sky particularly brilliant,
or beyond waters something intriguing
passing, perhaps no more than the play
of the sun descending, each far distant,
each just at the edge, the limit
of what the eye may yet perceive.
Or whether their attention was focussed
on an object directly before them,
no matter what the precise form,
a statue, a tapestry of biblical
or mythological heritage, a work of art
in whose creator he had also risen,
whose skills each had perfected, whose imagination
he had taken complete possession of.

5.

In the dark of a garden doorway, or when
on a bench in a park where weeping willows
cast shadows on a pond, in this
secluded silence a solitary figure sits
recalling perhaps scenes from childhood
and another whose thoughts are also filled with
the imagery, the music that such silence brings,
comes by the gate or the path and while passing,
while catching each others' eyes quickly,

by instinct almost, as athletes do
adroitly, flying, touching, then grasping
hands in the air, there comes over them
that recognition causing that memory too deep
to remember to reach to the surface,
the conviction that eludes even thought
for it is rooted as a tree is, as even
some flowers are, deep below the fields,
the forest covered with pine cones and needles:
the secret knowledge that he whom
they cannot name, has risen, is alive
within them, now holds them.
Or even in less romantic settings,
in crowded streets, subways, the workplace,
that instant between faces that is at once
too familiar and for some from experience
too elusive to give it attention,
transcribe it by thoughts.

6.

Out of dim reaches he rises,
has risen out of fields, out of stones
wherein without realizing it—for it had
been absorbed by them by customs, by
services all stemming from
the same recognition, that of
one prevalent, predominant reality—
those tilling the soil, shaping the stones
had imparted his presence. A wind
flies past, the leaves in the trees,
the stalks of wheat, of corn, of flowers
tremble. The clouds follow. The patterns within
the interior spaces the sun has cast on
the floor through tall, colored windows,

flicker, stay, then fade. Flowers surround
the base, creepers cling to the stones
of many a garden wall.
Inaudible, invisible, yet present.
A quality that those who live within—
the gardens, streets, towns—
who pursue whatever may be their
routine, accustomed to it, therefore
not aware of it, could not do
without. And they draw from it,
fill their need, as do the bees from
fuchsia bulbs hanging from terrace beams,
are fed by it and where they draw
the calm that sustains them in their sleep—
if they come, if they are disposed
to what in his essence he represents—
there is no resistance to this,
their even unconscious demand. Out of
such places, into their lives he rises.

7.

Sights have come from this
respect for what the unseen provides
in the spaces it has filled,
in the things that are seen, in the way
the cupolas gleam, the spires ascend,
the fields spread from the elevated town,
sights that cause even the casual visitors
to be uplifted, to rejoice.
                         With delight
they stride down into its midst, to squares
with tables along and outside colonnades,
with statues of personages of civic
responsibilities, heads of senate, of state,

others of classical myths or religious legend
displayed at appropriate locations.

They cross the bridges over canals,
wonder at the residences along them,
at the parks that embellish the rivers
and separate them from the crowded streets.
They recognize the benefit of this
for human habitation. They do not question
nor need to search out the imprint behind
without which such ambiance, such glorious
assertions of what remains hidden, although
in these and other expressions made evident,
could never be.
                    They visit
estates famed for their extravagance,
allées still neatly trimmed leading to
imposing villas, baroque fountains, water
cascading down and out of the mouths
of supply-limbed heroes and heroines.

But, no matter where they are, from where they look,
whether in town or out in the country,
they marvel at the perspectives filled with
agreeable sights, the natural order
and—where he has risen, had risen—
the absence of neglect.

                    8.

To those you near, those rare ones touched by
your spear, to whom you are evident behind
waters stirring as the desert sun ascends
from the Arabian sea; evident to them
within structures wherein sublimity

rises from unified complexities,
from harmonies as at the great cathedrals
of buttressed walls with towers and façades:
to them, those chosen, gifted ones, magnificent
are you in your forms assumed, munificent
to those who will not flourish, not complete
what the gifts bestowed on them compel them to,
will flounder, fail unless a closeness is
achieved. To them you impart yourself
into a depth they have not the means
to know, until a feeling they cannot help but
recognize, an absence, has set in. That this
cannot be so, committed as they have
become to you, that once in them you will not
let them go, they learn only gradually
until, by a magic particular to you,
no matter what they feel, conviction of
your presence is achieved.

9.

Out of dim reaches, he nears them
and from deep behind their sleep
when they ascend but have not yet
come fully back, when thus
they ascend from a depth
where they had been dissolved,
merged within the nothingness
that is presence without form—
this message just on waking,
just at the start of thoughts:
to keep alive what is alive,
has been and will always be,
but must be said, must be shown to be.

Out of dim reaches, when just
as sleep departs, the conviction
that there it was where happiness
resides, that it is rooted there,
deep in the depth, I hear just as
I wake, in thoughts that can then
occur, are not willed, rise up
on their own, this meaning that
was then and is now still distinct:

> *I am abstract, who am immediate,*
> *abstract who am immanent,*
> *immediate, immanent, who alone*
> *am real, am concrete,*
> *not abstract but more concrete*
> *than softest earth, the hardest elements*
> *with which those I command, those I*
> *have touched, have given shape to me*

★   ★   ★

High voices, voices at high range, in unison,
no melody, a chant, appeal varying only in
intensity like waves in accordance with
what is of greater will, of greater might;
voices, in unison, at a height where like
the waves dissolving into sprays,
a watery density in wind, in air,
the voices strive toward that extremity
where sound itself dissolves into
essence the ear can feel, no longer hear;
voices, in unison, aspiring toward sublimity,
toward where the changeless presence lies,
where every arm held upward in appeal
has reached; voices, high voices in
        high praise, in unison.

Geraniums

Seeing them late in the day
in the still brilliant light as though enshrined,
looking at them from my table across the room
in a window box or outside the open door in pots,
I could say that they remind me of so much,
so much I couldn't say precisely what.
They reveal then light's power to illuminate,
to bring out subtleties not only in
the colors, the beauty inherent in flowers,
but in the fuller picture, the narrow field,
fruit trees, the ivy-covered walls beyond them.
Such moments they bring to mind
when the thing looked upon displays
its mostly unobserved completeness,
appearing suddenly more than connected with,
related to, bonded with everything around it,
mysteriously made one, made perfect by
the great light, great distances of sky,
or of sea behind it. A boat half in the sand, one oar
in the water, a slight wind, slight rustling of waves,
a causeway with benches jutting out into the bay,
a fisherman seated along the edge,
his pole bent in the shape of a harp.

And he who observes this,
in whom now it lives,
who standing somewhat aside,
perhaps slightly above
on the paved road where cars are parked,
perceiving the details that combine into,
are parts of this harmonious assembly,
he cannot say just what it is, just what
the entire scene is symbolic of, except that

he is reminded of a perfection he has
in a manner as mysterious as is this
completeness, this light-drenched,
this strangely silent view before him,
always known, like a secret revealed
in this among other ways, as in a face
he may or may not have seen before:
this projection, sudden appearance of
a luminous reality he has more than once
been absorbed in, has more than once sensed
behind the happiest of dreams.

Father and Son at St. Benoît

After the vespers, when the monks sat
scattered throughout the great basilica,
head lowered, no matter what, how far
afield their thoughts, indrawn, each sunk
into himself, into silence, into and toward
the depth that has no chart, no measure,
that reach where sound begins
that is the heart's sole property,
pure chords that alone can stir
the reverent, attentive individual,
for there lies that assurance there,
the reality to which these men
have consecrated their lives.
Having surely absorbed as hymnal praise
the slender gracefulness,
the upward soaring columns, arches
in whose midst they now sat, they were,
indrawn, in their black cowls like
blackbirds on lawns, on branches, asleep
perhaps, at any rate, whatever their
purpose, in that pose resting,
at rest until some impulse, some hidden
stirrings make them move their wings.
In this silence, pervasive then
as water in a sea, as love can be
when neared attentively, in a manner
appropriate to it—a boy
of about ten stood clasped in his father's arms,
the father pressing the boy to him
as though reunited or while still
united but just before a parting that
must come. In this moment, this union,
the boy put his head upon the father's arm

and let it lay where it belonged,
loved just then by the love that in
this stillness, this silence behind
sound having filled the tall space
sanctified to it, was part of it
as water is in an ascending haze—
let his head rest in this embrace,
let it rest there for just a little while.

The River Serpent

1.

In a clarity as this, the views all of a piece,
the sky, blue hills, the river
winding to and from as far as the eye can see,
when unified like this, the angle shifts.
The serpent's languid turn and flow,
her murky color like the river's silt,
or the tree's bark like hardened mud,
her heavy spread and rhythmic breath
concealing the hiss that will in time
erupt (her head raised for the attack),
separates, intrudes. Side by side, her
heavy, spotted skin on our backs, her tail
wanting to wrap itself 'round our necks,
the dead stare of her unflinching eye
having wiped aside the shine of clarity.

2.

Cheated by her of whatever we have had
that we had come to love, all that
we strove toward, found, held, now gone
as though our former days had never been,
as though our happiest, saddest moments
when our mothers surprised us

with boundless attention and we felt
saddened by the sadness in their eyes;
as though our times in and walks through
the summer spas had never been; incredible!
as though our innumerable scenes of
intimacies had never been!

Cheated by her of nothing but all that
has ever been, no more, no less than that,
she weighs so heavily on us, we must
free her of her winding onward endlessly,
of her dependency on us, or
we cannot be, we cannot be.

3.

At a moment's lull, we see between
an opening in trees like a green gate,
a sunflower field vast as a yellow lake,
a streak, a glimmer in the sky; see in
the gatelike opening beyond the spreading
fields a strip into bright infinity,

stone terraces ascending like
broad steps on consecrated heights that lead
to ceremonial grounds up, up so high
and in so deep, our capacity for seeing
fully revealed those noble but receding forms
gives out, turns into invisibleness

back into ourselves. Is this not as
the serpent's path, back into ourselves
from where, as we looked upon the things
on either side of us, she came,
taking with her as she wound her
shadowy way, the clarity, pure sight
in which we first beheld her world?

4.

She is transparent now, continues as
she must, obedient, perhaps far more
than we shall ever be, to the source
from where, to where she flows. For,
the instant of the one decisive blow
her dense, her spotted, heavy skin,
her coat the color of mud, of bark,
took on illusion's diaphanous cloth—
pastels delicate as air, a gauze
no more substantial than a pollen dust—
the surface mirroring both, heaven's
countenance and the gross mien of the world.

Gesualdo

—to Bernard Rousseau

Liturgical music of the seventeenth century,
Gesualdo and some of his contemporaries,
no instruments, only voices, the voice as
instrument, as plea, as confusion, as lack
of comprehension from out of the depth, at

the passing, all the passings, of faces
like clouds, of a life young once, of a
contentment, intuneness with all there was—
village, brook, meadow, mountains—
this life that was once one's own

vanishing, vanishing, vanished almost.
No instruments but the voices finely tuned
to emotions which if they have not
already done so, will surely come,
will surely come upon one in this or

another chapel, in this or another country.
And there will be no applause only inward
acknowledgment and the knee bent.
Yesterday an angel came and brought me
strawberries late in the season but

the weather still warm enough for them
to grow, he brought a basket of them.
Although the father of two boys, he talked
as the child in him still might,
of the happiness he felt in the music,

the happiness of being one with all that is
outside yourself, vast as the clear autumn sky,

tall as the poplars already turned yellow.
This happiness of being truly and fully yourself.
Why shouldn't things be as they are?
Why must there be deception?

Like Marble

Art shaped for nothing but your response,
who recognize but transcend the forms
you activate, in whom the secret seethes,
sublime moments the landscape has
or sea when touched by rare luminescence,
the line where sea, or land, and sky are a
joined haze, a mist, a vaporous nothingness, a blinding

glow. . .

the colors on museum walls a brilliance
first revealed in dreams, music that aims
at nothing but concordance with your heart.
Long ago I sensed what you possess,
that there it is where it is actual.
A boy still, I had stood amazed by a sight
that although until then not faced
was as familiar as the mystery itself,
future known as the known past it held,
water pouring over you, your naked body tense with
the power to burst forth foaming,
glorious, youthful
and like the marble in imitation of you, ageless. . .

Yellow Wildflowers

Appearing one day
from where nor how I cannot say,
their presence alone is evidence.
How they have enhanced the field
rid of its weeds not long ago.
Just now through the open window
there is the smell of freshly cut grass
and from the room below
Fauré's Requiem on the radio.
As I look across and over them,
they, the smell of grass, the music trigger images:
Bourgeois extravagance,
a polished mahogany front door,
bell and nameplate in polished brass.
Intimations of intimacies.
A boy come with his class
for a swim in winter, stripped in the steam,
later descending the broad staircase
long looked after by a youth ascending.
Like now the flowers in the field across,
how often were there not those
who came up before me
as though wildly grown,
origin or even name
often unknown,
came and went as evidence,
as message that repeats itself
in the wind that brought these flowers here,
in the music that speaks of
transitoriness,
in feelings, in hints,
as when, now how long ago? we sped across a bay
but the waves too high, we could not

get off, returned to the pier,
walked back to the hotel
and when you left, I watched you go until
I could not tell you from
the others in the crowd. Or when,
and this with someone else,
we had come across each other on
a country road, you on your bike, I on foot,
a bird twittering, I remember,
just a single bird twittering.
And now, the Agnus Dei,
sheep bunched together on the meadow,
sunshine on the grass.
All this as evidence, as evidence of what?
That other side of things
we share but cannot hold?
Is what we must hunt
because it is too close,
what in the end we want?
Must we always want more
than what we see?
Odd that in a city built on water
the cobblestoned streets and squares
should impress us with its solidity,
a stone fountain trickling,
an unconcerned cat crossing.
This we accept. But have we learned,
have we learned to be content?
When at that village below the cliffs
you had gone down to the edge
and into the wind to test the waters,
I watched you from the higher pavement.
"Words are ambiguous" you had written,
"only feelings matter."
Never mind.

Never mind.
The sun has come down,
the sun now in those golden heads.

1995

Chiaroscuro

When, how far back? When I played
in the Augarten,★ grandmother watching me from
a bench, the chalky whiteness of
the gravel glistening in the sun
wiping away all that passed before me,
indistinct summonings in the haze,
by contrast the deep shade from trees so dark
I ran out from there fast as I could.
Or when, much older though still
in knee-socks and short pants,
one afternoon near an outdoor swimming pool
I had gazed in amazement at
an older youth under a shower head,
water pouring as long as he pulled
the chain attached to it
and I stood at a distance
barefoot on the grass. On the way home
crossing the bridge I leaned
over the railing and for a long time
looked below at the barges passing under it.
What other than their cargo did
they bring? I stared at
the hull, black, smeared and discolored
slowly moving by. From where did
they come and where will they unload?
When the maid had let me in she said
my friend, whom she referred to as
"your god" had telephoned. From my room
I caught, heart pounding, framed in
the window across, a glimpse of
a fully naked figure smooth and white
as statuary that had stepped quickly back
into the darkness letting the drapery

★ A former imperial park in Vienna

fall into place. Mirage or a true vision
from out of a past not yet mine,
the body shining forth aloof, sublime?
What was it in what lay hidden
that even then had hinted at
spectacular sounds and sights
beyond such I would hear and face,
would pursue and one day embrace?
Other than songs of yearning I had heard
at late sunset in the Prater as the Ferris wheel barely turned
and two figures had followed a third into
the dark of trees. Steadily, steadily,
the unheard drone no matter what
the melody, the distant glow even when
the dimness in the sky was gone and
one blackbird shrieked among the trees.
Or, years later, a scene that though in
a dream is vivid still: I come in
upon a square, in a house opposite
a single window is lit, dark the square,
the night sky alone glittering;
from all sides, from out of a deep
distance, there is music for which
there is no visible source. I near
the house, look in the window and stare at
two naked figures on a bed, bodies
so perfect only inspired masters
could have conceived of them, and
from there saw first expressed
a love that too desired to be real,
no human claim would keep,
no pleading retain. And later again
when having one day in class
on turning around looked straight into
a fellow student's eyes as though

finding there the self revealed
and knew what had amazed me then
would one day have to be my own,
what but apparitions followed
in the years ahead when the figure
having stepped forth from out of the dark,
looked at in daylight would always fade back;—
for it will not be trapped
what had infused itself in eyes
as pools, in limbs as grace,
each an apparition of the elusive self,
interplays of shade or, dark at
the edges, imperceptible light, intrusions
as when a legendary bird
on having achieved a god's desire, rose up
and disappeared back into the clouds.

★   ★   ★

Intrigued early on
by shapes and scenes against
a background dim or luminous,
a master's strokes on canvas—
and we may or may not have held
incarnate in the best of terms
what eludes and we will not possess—
we are moved in the end not so much
by what we have come upon as by
the feeling we are left with when
whatever provoked it is gone.

Despite dissolutions of
astounding figurations close at hand,
a foggy nothingness as that in dreams,
beyond the line where the sea moves in,
where oleanders bloom

and a steep slope dense with acacias
ascends into mountains that ring a port,
beyond its shady ridges, the land's blue
invisibleness begins and ends.

Aria

The tenderness in music
brings back moments I've shared
with some who are as I am,
as when in a darkened room
I had stood as though watching over him
at the head of the bed where he had lain
who on getting up and putting his hands on
my shoulders, giving his name, said:
"This I will not forget."
Or on an ocean crossing
when I had found myself up on deck
next to someone I had seen but never met,
and looking out on
the brilliance of light on water
and the harbor ahead
remembered an arrival by sea
that I had dreamed
and on turning toward him
who had also turned toward me,
saw the welcome that had awaited me there
and the radiance around us now
as a luminous oneness between us.
Or when sharing a similar look
with someone just passing by
in a park, a car, a street
or while crossing it,
or when opposite or next to someone on a train,
there may have come upon us,
or risen up in us
a tenderness that is not realized
unless reflected in the other
through whom we may at last have met,
if only for the briefest instant,

what was long desired
because for long foreknown—
a benevolence, musical, intimate,
whose source we cannot name,
whose cause we recognize
in each other's eyes.

Earlier, out on the terrace, I heard
from deep within the dense acacias
now in fragrant white bloom, a different tune
from birds singing forth lustily
this courting month of June.

In Himself Absorbed

He realized as he sat on the train
and looked at the young man opposite him,
that what had years back provoked
a longing in him, did so no more.
Odd that in the face of someone young
he should then have sensed a permanence,
a place where time had ceased to be,
where trees stood still and a small boat
tied to the bank lay as though blind
in unreflecting waters.
It had beckoned him as nothing else.
But earlier in the day
as he had passed at the bottom of
a long flight of steps
two actors rehearsing for a play
and he had just descended from
the city's highest hill* where he
had come upon a blackfaced mime
mimicking motionlessness like the absence of time,
and directly after had stepped into
a crowded Sacré-Coeur where at vespers
an organ played, a choir sang;
and later had sat into the night
opposite Notre-Dame brightly lit—
and various and far-flung across
ancient coasts and rivers had been
the scenes that had instructed him—:
he knew he had by then
in himself absorbed,
in himself retraced
the distant glimmers from that place,
the stillness and deep
remembrance in another's face.

---

* Paris, Montmartre

Disarrangement

The trees' height told a great age
and that some were not fully leafed, split,
chunks torn from them, of storms, disease.
Their denseness shaded the canal
freckling the water and the path along it.
A magpie skimming the surface, fluttering up
marked the silence where he had come to walk.
A boat that fishermen might use to row across
or to spots where fish gathered en masse,
lay half in the water, half in sludge,
another further down moored to a post.
Odd to see boats with no one in them,
emptied of the thoughts of men that had
possessed them and as he passed them
he thought of himself as emptied of
moments that had possessed him, of journeys,
of gusts at sea, of changes made,
of houses left, of loves too swiftly had.
And yet in this disarrangement of the scene—
trees irregularly leafed, trunks halved,
some slanted, bent, others reaching upward from
the water like accusing arms—
there rose in him from deep within
what he would not be emptied of:
a steadiness that not like
events has come and gone
but that now as he walked on
took in with equal equanimity
the flutterings and shrieks of birds,
the seeming motionlessness of water lily leaves,
the stillness and disorder in the trees.

The Poem, Ousson-sur-Loire

As I got out of my car,
heard organ music coming from
Ousson's chapel and looking in
saw a woman alone in a pew
and then stepping down into the garden
the river's surface ahead
silken and shining, the light
not aggressive but spreading
the good news it carries,
I knew that the poem was there.
For as it stirs, as it rises
the poem within is the poem hidden in
the things that are seen,
and the empty boat with mast so fine
it might have been drawn with pencil on paper,
was one site where the poem lay,
and the man on a bench
and his dog sniffing was another,
as was the light's glimmer
around the edges of bushes and trees
bunched together on both sides of the river,
and where the river drops abruptly
and young paddlers maneuvered their canoes skillfully,
the sparkle the water creates
as it rushes down and seething leaps up.
For the poem within
must present evidence
of whatever lends impact to a scene,
the dim interior a door opens on
where a woman's thoughts alone in a pew
mingle with solemn chords whose source
she feels but cannot see.
And it must provoke

reflections on happiness caught
but never kept, the moments years back
a man looking out on the river's bright calm
ponders as he sits on a bench.
It must fill in the boat
with cargo and crew or the owners cruising,
the mast sturdy and the sails rising—
and gladly will it grant paddlers
their exuberant claims of youth,
shouts of joy and risks
as their boats jump down
the river's seething fall.

Six Days in Prague

Disappearance sweeps over me.
Mozart's *Laudate Dominum* in St. Nicholas' Church,
traces fade, the ripples from the boats
that pass,
      the water flows,
            the water stays.
As I relive some of the scenes
and recall their sense of being deeply in place,
the intimacy with streets, outlying woods
that I once had comes back to mind.
Like Prague, Vienna is surrounded by
hills on one side and as a boy
I would often sit there by a pond
and watch the swans in a park
where, when it was private, young Loris★
had walked with friends and I,
not knowing this then, took in
what must have also affected them,
murmurs among the willows' trembling leaves,
their shadows flecking the water,
a swan, rising slightly, shaking its wings.
Substance-less as thoughts,
such scenes some recent ones called forth,
as are now those I'd come upon this time:
the elderly woman on the tram
hearing us speak French, no doubt
reminded of her former days, smiling
and saying a few words to us as we got off;
the swans in a cove under the bridge
we crossed to the old Town, to its
steep streets, squares, churches, castle on the hill;
from the music conservatory's open windows
the sounds of a violin and piano team

★ Hugo von Hofmannsthal

practising, a soprano repeating trills,
the crowds waiting at the Town Hall's tower
to see the mechanical figures appear on the hour;
the tower, castle, cathedral and others of
the city's main sights, lit up at night.
Six days of newly acquired images
now nothing but the essence in which
they were conveyed to us when they
like the sight-seeing steamers
crammed with tourists approached
and disappeared below the bridge.

Returned, back in my room
familiarity seems to postpone
this fleetingness. I turn
to music, to Schubert's, Beethoven's late piano sonatas,
sadness the only just response
to disappearance, the absolute end
that each thing has, and hear in them
lyrically evoked
the tolerant acceptance of this intolerable fact.
Laudate Dominum
     traces fade,
        the water flows,
Laudate Dominum
     the water stays.

And I have stood behind each scene
each time as it reflects itself on me,
have received its forms and,
when struck by its appearance,
saw what the forms suggest;
have stood behind and
unwilling to accede
have long looked back,

have kept its startling impact,
and that which within me takes
all in, is there, unchanged
and present as the water is
when the boats have long gone past,
when the swans under the bridge
in agitation rise and beat their wings.
Laudate Dominum the soprano sings,
remembrance descends,
recognition stuns the audience.
The doors open. It is sunny. It is
late afternoon. Briefly
the crowd departing lingers on the steps.

Portrait

A portrait of myself
of more than thirty years ago
bought by a friend
who willed it to a friend
who has willed it to me,
now hangs in my bedroom/study
facing my desk. Drawn in crayons,
the colors mostly subdued blues,
my head resting on the right hand,
often my pose when listening.
A pensive look; too sad, some say,
as if I knew then what I would see
in it now.
              A long procession
of figures receding in the background
bright as in a surrealist painting,
my mother listening to an opera
affected by the lovers' fate
and I, in the same room with her,
helpless to console her.
A boyhood friend I had scorned,
another I had preferred
who when we were grown
but hadn't met in years,
leaned over me as I sat
in a darkened theater
waiting for the film to start.
And so many others
and events all fixed in
memory's compelling tones of
an unnamed happiness lost,
and the sights reflecting this,
as when even as a youth

I had sensed a desperate want
in figures embracing in a doorway
or disappearing behind shrubbery;
or when observing from my window
in a room across the courtyard
an aged father caring for
an adolescent daughter,
just the two of them at table behind
the undrawn curtain.

                              Or years later
on travels, long journeys,
when on a walk by the sea
in the dim darkness spotting the stranger
who would know me instantly,
would know why, a few steps away,
I would stop to look back.
What, in the end, are travels all about,
at least what have mine been all about
if not to regain, be close again
to that unspecified loss,
the promise of retrieval
contained in sceneries, vistas strongly marked,
from terraces high above sloping flowery fields,
from classical hillsides
possibilities for a union with
the great good gained
long before memory began,
long before the streets,
the dark and narrow, broad
and tree-lined streets
where I had been at home
were gone.

In the portrait, in its subdued blues
the artist caught in that wistful look

what I had to have learned too well
even by then, nothing lasts, nothing can.

                    The coasts recede,
swift, billowing clouds, the earth.
Not the confrontations, face to face
nor an accord of place—
deep in the bright far end
in the unchanging glow
solace gained alone remains,
                              recoveries
for which travels were begun.

At the Beginning of the End of Day

The sky white, the water clear,
the sunset's red in the river and canal,
gardens, houses, trees look scrubbed
in the descending light.
Earlier as I came up the garden steps,
hearing music, the sounds of
permanence in it as in his words,
I wondered how it might have been
had Bach been performed for him
in whose stone-like pose
all sorrows and all joys dissolved.
Now at the beginning of
the end of day, what would I say
could I sit once again
before him as I did
when flying foxes hanging in the palms
took wing and rushed off
into the sunset toward the sea?
Language, sounds and landscapes washed
when thoughts were cleansed
and torments wiped away.
In a photo of myself
in Venice on my way back
in early evening at a table at San Marco,
a smart scarf tucked into my jacket,
I have the look of someone cleansed.
Glorious had been the entrance
down the canal, water splashing against
the base of Ducale and other palaces.
Vivaldi and imagined trumpet sounds
emblazoning the air.
And elsewhere, stairs
to pillars, seats of the gods,

lampposts along the river and
in parks, sharp and clean
as though mirrored in
the source of pure reception.
Now at the beginning of
the end of day, the water and
the things around it
shining briefly in late light's clarity,
what would I say, knowing that no
appeal will make appearance stay;
what would I ask, having learned
that nothing can be changed
of what was long ago decreed?
Unresolved desires lingering on,
besmirched by ponderings
I would not ask, I would just sit
on the ground and listen, listen
as the bats fly off in a cloud.

Three Autumn Moods

Opposite the river
in the garden below the village church
a man is raking leaves.
Along the bank
and just beyond it
two fishermen stand at the edge of
a causeway formed by rocks,
another sits on a raft,
another stands in the river
his figure elongated by
his shadow in the water.
In a wooded patch
a man is getting rid
of fallen twigs by fire.
High overhead a flock of geese.

The man raking leaves,
another's body a shadow in the water,
the fire, the flying geese—
what are they to
the disconsolate figure walking past
but signs of
transitions on command?

Empty fishing boats
tied to posts in the river.
A gull sits perched on one
then flies off.
A racing team in colorful canoes
is swiftly moving up
to where boulders create a drop.

On the bank a woman on a bench
looking through binoculars
anticipates their jumps.
Two girls and a big black dog
pass me on the road
followed by two women bicycling.

I have passed them, seen
the boats, canoes, binoculars,
the bird disappearing into a sky
the color of its feathers,
have seen them fade away
into awareness strolling past,
an indifferent presence
detached like light
on water, like the wind
ruffling it.

High above a widespread meadow
a small plane performs for
an airshow in the next town.
A dog running past me ignores me.
The river follows its destination.
Asleep, it will sink into myself.

Behind the pilot's stunts,
behind the dog sniffing its way back,
behind the river following its course without choice;
hidden away from comprehension
a dictate lurks in its own domain.
Nothing admitted there
but needed rest at each return.

A shine in the room on waking.
A hum of deep male voices,
inward chants of solitude.

The Park

"Philosophy is, strictly speaking, a homesickness." — *Novalis*

"...we feel at home nowhere except on the way to the total and essential." — *Heidegger*

As a boy
crossing the Augarten
troubled by classroom thoughts
and in view of the chestnut trees
that formed stately allées
and of glimpses from there of lawns and flower beds
I formulated a term
for what to my mind then
could not only have had residence in heaven
but looking at what surrounded me
was surely everywhere
and as I made my way to school
(though not on my return),
addressed that as:
"Du Himmlischer Alles Gott"
(Thou Heavenly Everywhere God)

Or when up in the attic
looking from the dormer window toward
the Wienerwald where it rises above the Danube,
it was in the distance
that my connections lay,
celebratory phrases, rhythmic words
stored in the invisibleness it held.

Or whenever answering the doorbell
to beggars or visitors,
once they had gone, the effect of
their appearance remained,

or of nostalgic melodies
hummed by my father along with
a childhood friend,
or of my own new friend's affectionate gesture

never the actuality
but the unsaid meaning,
a reference to slumbers
in hideouts along sewers,
to horses on stormy days
rearing up in agitated fields,
to tedious hours in *cheders*,
to happiness regained
in that touch of an arm around my shoulder.

———

After days of desolation—
of recognizing and regretting
patterns about which I can do nothing—
while finding myself talking to friends
clearly as though it were actually happening,
of the advantages of living in a city
imbued with at least a former awareness of
transcendent glories;
or when discovering as I enter
a cell-like room
someone not expected
and the incontrovertible fact that
the presence, as deeply desired as it is needed,
is once again before me, comes to me—
in the shape of someone both male and female,
someone who turns from one into the other—
and I know as I wake that the love
that is neither one nor the other,

present in both
rises beyond the shape it possesses
to a residence it alone inhabits
and yet shines to us through the eyes of those
who in Rilke's words, are the beginning of hearts
—"Die Ihr der Anfang der Herzen scheint"—
sings to me through the works and words of those
informed by their sworn allegiance:
it is finally once again that love
that holds me then for at least
as long as I can ward off awakening.

———

I say as I wake,
there I want to be,

> *O that we may rest there, stay there,*
> *held by what, in us*
> *from beginning to end, is ours!*

nothing equals it
though much points to it,
patterned, classic lawns on either side of me,
a pond from where at its edge
children pilot their boats,
a dream in which
I welcome a friend long dead at my door,
the harvested field I drive past at sunset,
the wheat bound in rolls. . .

even the music I listen to
as such sights come back to me
cannot equal it:
                              the times when

260

having reached there
after twenty-three days
by ship,
          I climbed the stairs
opened the gate
and that which has
          neither birth nor death

looked at me

————————

Has haunted me, in faces mostly,
even before I had confronted it,
when young, not long in a new land,
in some I passed in streets still strange to me,
a look in which I felt not loss
but a belonging common to us both.
And afterwards
in some I glimpsed behind me,
one afternoon in Estoril's flower-filled terrace café,
or in a dear friend's direct stare
I had no choice but to refuse,
and later in his invisible self
that detached itself from him
and I was free to join with mine
as we walked back to our hotel
during the Bayreuth Festival.
Or in some of nature's displays,
white blossoms strewn across my lawn
that only days before had grown
to bell-shaped flowers on the catalpa's wide leaves;
or even at such drastic times when
long ago inflicted wounds rose up,
cast-offs and dust collected there

challenged at last. And in all sorts of attempts
that might bring me close to it,
on journeys, meetings by chance,
views of the sea from mountain peaks
bare as the eagle's head
that flies from it.

———

This morning,
awake but not yet claimed by
the first sight I caught
of foliage flickering through half-closed shutters
on the tile floor,
I rested, rested long
in the deeper than sleep nothingness.
Later in the day,
back from having gone for bread,
hearing a Schubert sonata on the radio—
sadness inherent in transitoriness,
in daily life,
happiness needed but elusive as
light's flickering,
as promise in a stranger's eyes—
I thought back on my solitude at twenty
walking by a river
in an alien and impersonal city
begging for aid from
compassionate spirits
to come to me,
to hold me and keep me embraced
as out from their own great depth
I might rise into the day.

———

Love I asked for as I woke
not such as I have
but the one I lost
when the things of this world
began to come toward me
advanced toward me
and I was not consoled.

———————

It flows, flows, fades—
impressions we harbor, recollect
when sounds or sights
harmonious as those we had absorbed
take us back to when confronting them
whether we stood behind an ornate gate
or viewed the gardens from a greater height.
"It must be abstract" Stevens said,
must be, because it is; and Crane to Emily:
"You who. . . fed your hunger like an endless task."

To be stirred is not enough,
the most intimate of recognitions
a good occasion might have brought
—of all needs the most desired—
at far remove from us.
Lampposts are lit
and we move on
before the gates are closed.

The brush on my cheek
when I was in my teens,
by touch awakened then
to the intimacy of
what in its nature is elusive,

has come back to me
in sounds, in someone's face
in a room, in a crowd,
more often than my bewilderment,
the first of this sort,
when my friend
when we were forced to flee, left
and I remained back on the track
as the train pulled out.

How they continue to affect us,
long after, back in our rooms,
how they bring and brought to mind
the radiant colors
in the stained-glass windows
in the lofty dim interior
from where we had just come,—
those amply filled, formal flower beds
behind the Cathedral at Bourges.

———

We go there, stroll there, sit there
to recapture moments
that not only as we remember them
but even as they happened
were charged with a meaning to which
we can assign no adequate significance
as though come to us from where
meaning is beyond definition,
a brightness in the sky,
a sudden darkening,
wild geese departing,
on a raft tied to a post in the river
a man sits fishing from a chair.

And as each flashback occurs—
through open windows
the sounds of a piano
from down the street
in a town no longer ours—
removed where we are,
sounds of steps on the gravel,
sounds of flutters in trees,
removed as then we are from
other concerns:
the recognition, retrieval of
a happiness, a cause we cannot name.

———

And just now as I was leaving the bakery
and caught in a flash—
        as though of a photo
        taken by the invisible
        in accord between us—
the appealing impression of someone entering,

I thought of the many similar exchanges
when you were young,
glimpses, quick recognitions
that happened often in crowds
or in a room in someone standing across from you,
in whom this need was as much alive
as it was then in you,
to retrieve that locality
no designation will reveal
though suggest by such elements as
long allées dimming toward a brightness at the deep end,
benches along the side, empty stone basins
wherein are posed

figures of vague classical significance,
nymphs, water gods, Neptune perhaps, a place
of sharp shadings of light,
of a transcendent order
where he, like you,
was sure that he had been,
but when and where beyond recall.

So often,
and to what account
other than this provoking flare-up,
you could never tell.

It is early autumn,
the afternoon sunny,
if possible
I walk daily along the canal that follows the wide river between dense
                                        acacias and pastures;
a cow at a trough watches me come past, then bends down to drink again;
other than this herd and at the farm a dog barking
there is no one about.

I follow a narrow pebbly path, one of two along a strip of grass,
the water, spotted perhaps from leaking barges, though not stagnant, barely
                                        moves;
the shades of green
varied by the sun lingering lazily as though conforming to
the autumn mood, on the trees, meadows, in patches on the water,
reveal no more than
their greenness,
the entire sun-streaked scene—
a film of projected luminous nothingness
in deep harmony with my solitariness—
spreads before me.

———

He looks upon the two dogs frolicking
and is at one with them. Nothing can
separate the little boy of two or three
from what appears in front of him,
especially the tumbling of dogs, of one
upon the other, this oneness with
another that he has had
and one day will have to have again,
so natural, so complete is it just then,
his wide-open trusting eyes reveal.
His little sister comes to take him by the hand
back to the bench where his grandmother sits
chatting with a friend. It is
the square at the Place Dauphine,
the trees, leaves, windows below roofs
speckled with late light lingering,
a place, a moment of simple intimacies,
of a belonging akin to where
not long ago he had been taken from
and one day will reflect back upon,
that surfacing will cast its shine on him—
and has not changed
and will not cease to summon him
from deep, from deep within.

———

Between sleep and waking
awake not yet fully to the room,
the baldachin above the bed
characteristic of the house
where long ago (they say) a king had slept,
nor to the luminous Provençal dawn between the drapes,
but entirely to

a condition from within,
a force made up of
affection for and from
a stranger I had now come to know
and of the effect on me that day
of olive groves we passed,
of once medieval villages perched on hills,
of a garden of simples adjacent to
a ducal palace still in use,
and of everywhere the sun on stones.
Between sleep and waking
the sense of that which lasts,
which has not come to be but is,
and not as days later
on my return on waking,
the unalterable fact—
intolerable, unacceptable—
that all that had that day occurred,
all that had brought me back
to this inward force of joy and ease—
house and talks and meals with friends,
and everywhere the sun on stones—
has disappeared, has had
to disappear.

———

The background

ignored

until forced by circumstance

                              to turn

we look behind

and are eased back
to where we have been
and would want again to be

shadows of long lines of trees
swallows flying out from there
and figures moving away from there
in the distance touched by sun

for love
for the love of one
we barely know.

★ ★ ★ ★

Recently visiting Vaux le Vicomte,
the château of Louis XIV's tax collector,
the garden's strict formality
recalled for me
how even at the age of ten
on my way to school
I had appealed to naturalness,
not wanting to be pulled away
by subjects that didn't interest me,
by answers I didn't have,
by the snickerings of those who did,
and having seen the naturalness
of long lines of trees,
their shadows absorbing me,
had pleaded for
a freedom such as theirs,
having sensed by then
that harmony is natural in man.

Perhaps Louis XIV confronted by
Lenôtre's ingenuity

in extracting from nature
the harmony in which
the genius in him had instructed him,
saw this great achievement as
a just expression of his own majesty
and proclaiming his minister a probable thief
threw him in prison
took it away from him,
installed his court in it
and proceeded to build Versailles.

————

In the midst of nature's
inherent harmony,
in Parc Monceau a young mother feeds
her three-week-old baby,
two elderly women walk slowly past
wide lawns, tiered flower beds and white statuary;
on a path circling the park
joggers run, do push-ups, stretch limbs.

Hidden although expressed,
aware of it even as a boy
or just recently
in mountainous Auvergne. . .

while all we observe
has been and is absorbed in us,

it alone persists

in music informed by it—

music
that restores us to scenes,

appearances
that only yesterday
seemed fulfilled and permanent.

———

References provoked
of gardens lost but not abandoned,
connections retained
whether it be by horns to announce,
accompany a hunt,
or the clarinet to soothe
the innocent into the night,
or the violin, piano reflecting on
a childhood walk past gardens in bloom,
days by the sea and a cloudless sky,
whether cantatas a bishop ordered
or a prince elector as a birthday ode,
serenades to court, to entertain
peasants at a harvest feast:
each grown where ties
to hidden harmonies remain.

———

Why else did some poets turn backwards
to create in their minds
conditions that had made
for harmony, for an
approximation of beauty lost
but in that Hellenic ideal
not abandoned,
or when in rococo Austria
an empress ruled
and order was sustained

to which forests, farmsteads, gardens and statuary
still testify. . .
was that not
a way of getting at
the early gardens—
seats of stone the color of sunlight,
shadowless lanes—
they retain within themselves
and now glimpse in worn façades,
now catch in passing silhouettes?

The oneness that he believed
had once united
rulers with the ruled,
poets and philosophers with
their followers in open markets, public baths,
he for one (the Alexandrian Greek) sought to regain
among lethargic places—
narrow streets and by the sea outdoor cafés—
and for relief from
the longing that his reading and
the ancient city of his birth
had induced in him,
went to find it in
encounters with young men.

———

They cannot name just what it is
that they are really after
when they have come to the darkened rooms
where they can strip and turn into
their shadowy selves
pursuing their desires.
Once, way back, they'd heard

a song they cannot forget;
cannot forget the face they had glimpsed
once in a dimly lit street.
Out there we're thought of as
important but have not gained
and will not gain
what we had once possessed.
A happiness a song provoked,
a face suggests—
the bright vision of
a land submerged
that draws them to
the darkened rooms
where it lies buried in
—and beckons from—the flesh.

  To be among those who yearn
to be among those who feel themselves
deprived
deprived of what once they must have had
but cannot extract
as image, as event
though deep in memory
at the root of desire
it lies, spurs on
pursuits, spurs on
letdowns, even tears

in their daily lives
they can find no reference
in what surrounds them
to a closeness they remember
a happiness they cannot define

and they have come to seek it in
the only access available to them. . .

To be with them
to be one among them
who having stepped out of
having left their world behind
have sought refuge and release
in darkened rooms
is to regain
by contact, by intimacies
intimate moments
for which there is no adequate description
except that
it may bring them—
for however brief a time—
closeness to that
which will never desert them.

    Shining like the sun in an empty sky
moments that had absorbed
views of landscapes, rivers, towns,
details of interiors, lavish, sparse,
moments that having absorbed everything
are moments shining as nothing but themselves,
moments of nothing
moments beyond remembrance
empty and vast. . .

as when
some in their boyhood
wading in a brook
entangled with

tree shadows trembling in
the sun-spotted surface down to the silt,
lost all thought
lost in the memory of something they couldn't remember
but wanted to cling to. . .

or brought to the open window
by the sounds of a familiar tune
and spotting in the window opposite
a youth's fully naked body
behind a thin curtain
disappearing as it appeared,
such perfection in human form
for the first time seen
leaving a lasting impression
as though what had flashed across
and had enticed the boy was
a promise from the home that is lost
but never known. . .

   Desire having come to rest—
the way that waves touching the coast
lie flat when the storm clouds have rolled
across and all is calm—after desire,
the peace that follows attainment,
the moment that follows restlessness.
Something beyond the touch, beyond
the edge where desire has led you,
something pristine, something
beyond any claim has touched you.
Though you have no clear concept
of what or where it is wherein
at desire's end you now expand,

you have at times been convinced
that it exists, as when
after a steep descent you've come upon
a bay, a sea flat, azure, without end,
or when as a boy startled
to recognize in a quick young male
your own familiar form. Now reposing
in where you belong and long to be,
early days come back, whispers in
the silver leaves of wintry trees,
a face in a pond distorted by
the wind. Brought back by the body's touch
to this your deepest self
you don't now want to have to think
of what must come next,
that you will soon rise to descend
to streets you had rushed down before,
that you will then retake,
headlights cramming lanes,
pedestrians swarming.

★　★　★　★

Unmistakable in its effect,
not captured in the eyes it floods,
images, words it illuminates,
music that strikes because of it,
fields arranged in accord with it,
intimate as nothing else is,
gripping us as nothing else does,
august, impersonal, eluding us:

for what but for closeness to
that innermost core outwardly expressed
have I ransacked figures, forms,

out-of-the-way rooms for yield of it—
what but for the love it holds,
what but for the love it gives!

Given off by all we see and hold,
that no one holds nor sees, but o
for the one in whom it dominates,
the moments sought for such remembrance!

The gates have closed,
or as they close
stillness descends
that is a part of
that other side of things
where those who had sat
or walked between lawns and trees
turn into the essence of
their sleep, joined there
to dissolving shapes, to harmonies
that they would never want to leave.

———————

Children as they are close to it still
do not have to transcend their world to remain in it,
scooping up sand and pebbles into pails
they had carried with them to the park,
or cuddling a parent
driving over hills in a storm,
access to it not yet lost
children are not removed as we became
when such trusts were intermittent
and before long gone altogether
except for rare and momentary recollections
that seemed to occur beyond any reason

like the meeting in a dream
with someone loved,
by whom we are loved,
whom we have never known.

As the train pulls out of a station,
as we look back and see the huge suspended clock,
as we look back at what we have left,
at what we have had to leave,
it is easily missed
the turn we would have had to take,
the turn not easily taken,
the turn embedded
even as we depart—
the promise of it
in an assenting look
we recall as having been
directed at us in passing.

———

When what matters most has left us
and that alone which never leaves
remains. . . and we think back
to where our thoughts cannot reach,
think back as well
to much that brought us fulfillment
but held no permanence,
when only the thought that continues
sustained us,
the sea that was there
but not the ships
nor the ancient craft
in the deeply shaded canal.
I had reached

where I needed to be
and what was said has stayed on
but the occasion is gone.
Even the changes
caused or come about by themselves
were no more than
waves in the sea,
unobserved as they occurred
but not when what we had been accustomed to
was no more.
Like the eagle's shadow
across the darkening valley
from a terrace by the sea.
And when we wake
and we have been
where nothing changes. . .

*oh when we wake
and we have been
where nothing changes. . .*

Men chained to each other
dragging a boat upstream through mists,
think back to the one place
they want to remember,
the one place they feel
but cannot envision in detail.

———

The scenery changes,
not the reference.
Scenes there are
that provoke in us
the place where we have been

but cannot name,
a happiness
though to say that we
are happy where we are
does not equal it.
In a sudden burst of sun
tops of trees, roofs
dissolving—
the cupola golden even when
mists are not dispelled—
turn us back to
the source of our fondness
that art
and music most of all
approximates.
The child led by
the mother across the esplanades
keeps looking back at us
in fascination.
And we too
far far from childhood,
how easily we are turned
inward and backward—
as we cross a street
watch the traffic
or seated outdoors at a café
look at others passing.

—Behind what we have seen,
behind where we have been,
the tall iron gates
and park beyond
remain as always in a haze.

————

280

Present in me earlier
before awakening and
awakening aware and glad of it
then later
when coming in upon this scene
the river shallow
the exposed stones and pebbles

     saying

the water calm
here and there slight ripples from the fish below the surface

     saying

a few scattered flat empty fishing boats tied down near the bank

     saying

one fisherman standing in the river
the water just up to his boots

     saying

the entire vast openness—
sky water trees and bushes on both sides of the river,
the terns gathered on exposed sandbars—

     saying

no name
the presence here
nameless

although in childhood

as I walked down the gravel path between
a long row of trees leading to
the park's imposing imperial building
old and pale as its ghost,
having left my other world behind
named
named that to which even then
as a boy of ten
I knew that I belonged.

———————

Again the water
as I had often looked down on
from flowery heights
gardens terraced and descending

again the unearthly quiet
on the water
where the river is as wide as a lake,
the visible surface
the color of invisibleness,
the color of invisibleness
provoking a longing
that was with me
even when as a boy
on my way to matters forced on me
I crossed a park
that even then
seemed saturated with
the invisibleness that water has
when the day is more than luminous,
the green of water, of trees in the thin light
thin and shadowless.

There there
the deepmost sorrow cries

there there
the music I love says

there where the stillness of water hangs
between the palms

there where
awaited by the nameless
I had ascended

there there
o there

So Fleet, So Infinite

I don't want the past.
Each moment a betrayal.
What is now is what persists
as it did even when magnificence appeared.
For those who had wandered from afar,
for what now had been returned to them
—(if visible, which it wasn't,
a column of lightening)—
prostrate in the dusty courtyard,
and from the dead, hosannas in the palms.
Nowness that lasts
even if the sacred grounds
have not.
And of the brilliant terraces,
ascending roadlights
as the boat approached Cannes,
I Solisti Veneti in the stadium's horseshoe setting,
the familiar, ancient tunes renewed
and penetrating,
and in the risen mist the prevailing,
invisible presence of the sea.
Now descending. Now lifting.

now descending   now lifting

They were not there, though they
sat next to me at a Paris café,
a science student from eastern Russia,
his bearded friend, a young Italian poet,
two American women asking for
the Flore's menu so thick I took it to be a book,
weren't there not because they'd left
but because that which is there

284

possessed them, made of them not the past
but what has its root in me
as do the crows
when tomorrow they will fly across
my house in Châtillon,
or the young wrens in June
when I sit out in the back
and they are hidden in the trees and sing.

hidden in the trees and sing

In mid-July a rainy afternoon in Joigny
and dinner at a restaurant along the Yonne,
opposite the river's small port
where some river cruisers and private boats were berthed.
What persists and where? Of sights such as
the wealthy elderly couple advised by
the chef of the day's best choices;
or as we were about to leave
of the group of young, late diners coming in and ordering
a bottle of champagne; or of when
earlier in the day, we had stood in front of
la Vierge au Sourire, the charged silence at
l'église St-Thibaut, her smile that cuts across
centuries:—only what has been there
all along behind all these.
Only that.
We cannot think about
nor even recollect.
               The boats
we took away with us
dimly lit as we look back.

dimly lit as we look back

And yet. And yet. A presence beyond these,
if not the form it had, nor forms surrounding it—
in the courtyard gathered, or proceeding in a line,
white-clad along the coast, along the water's edge—
stays on. The Ever Present One,
The Invisible One who absorbing all
had also made them vanish, those torments
opposing the light that no one sees. As he had
predicted, grouped around him
near the cowshed in the shadow of
the immense pepper-tree, "they will
come up but they come up
to be destroyed" and rode
with me, behind me as if in a descended jeep
across farms and forests,
shadows shifting, darknesses behind the tangled,
tumbled, bent, split woods shifting back
and forth, furies released and battling,
raging within. And "On" he commands, and "on, to fight, to
                                        fight"
until, deep in the night, from ages back,
(how many lives? how many lives?)
horses rose jumping over hurdles,
three barriers in succession
and you, afterwards, lying flat on the ground

joy to have merited the pain

lying flat on the ground among
smoke lifting from the cinders
into the pure light of
daylight. . . and the Presence
stretched out across earth and the heavens
returned to where it had never left.
And you, you stand in It now,

back to where
you had never not been
and look back
when you had stood there
and tremble. . .

    and tremble

               so fleet,
so fleet thou wert when present—
so infinite (intimate) *when gone* ★

               2002

★ Emily Dickinson, #788

A Note on the Author

Arthur Gregor, born in Vienna, fled with his family to the United States at the outbreak of World War II, eventually settling in New York. After serving as a senior editor in the trade department of The Macmillan Company during the 1960s, he joined the English faculty at Hofstra University, where he set up Creative Writing and Publishing Studies programs and was, for seven years before his retirement in 1995, Poet-in-Residence. Since his first appearance in *POETRY* in 1947, for which he was awarded the magazine's First Appearance Prize, his poems have been published widely in most of the leading outlets for poetry. For the past twenty years he has spent part of the year in France's Loire Valley, and in 1998 moved from New York to Paris.

Also by Arthur Gregor

POETRY

Octavian Shooting Targets
Declensions of a Refrain
Basic Movements
Figure in the Door
A Bed by the Sea
Selected Poems
The Past Now
Embodiment and Other Poems
Secret Citizen
The River Serpent and Other Poems
That Other Side of Things

MEMOIR

A Longing in the Land

FOR CHILDREN

The Little Elephant (Photos by Ylla)
1 2 3 4 5 (Photos by Robert Doisneau)
Animal Babies (Photos by Ylla)

PLAYS

Fire!
Continued Departure
The Door is Open

290

"Poems that are, of their kind, almost perfect...At his best Mr. Gregor has not only gravity but an enviable purity."
— Daryl Hine, *Poetry*

A BED BY THE SEA (1970)

"In this, as in former collections, Gregor's tone and the color of his thought are so consistent he might be writing one continuous poem, the Song of Himself."
— May Swenson, *The Southern Review*

"Poems of the purest lyricism...These poems are almost transparent; rarely an image breaks the metaphysical mode where the poet sings of a worldly-unworldly universe."
— *Milwaukee Journal*

SELECTED POEMS (1971)

"The accuracy and integrity of his memory invests even a small moment with exquisite dimension...his natural talent cannot not orchestrate the perceptions into word-things of beauty.... Under the colloquial surface, whose texture Mr. Gregor has modulated with ever more impressive control, book by book, lives faith in ecstasy and the sharp anguish of loss and regret."
— F. D. Reeve, *Poetry*

"[The book] becomes the record of the adventures of the soul among the shoals and hazards of contemporary life. Mr. Gregor's technique and language serve him admirably. The lines are thoroughly transparent.... His work is free of harshness, violence, stridency... it is the authentic voice of a poet assaulted on so many sides that his only defense is the interior world he has erected to save him."
— Thomas Lask, *The New York Times*

"*Selected Poems* offers the reader an especially intriguing spiritual and artistic autobiography.... Well within the tradition of Keats, Whitman, and Frost."
— Christopher Collins, *The Nation*

"Few writers have sustained such purity of intention combined with virtuosity of form, or have grown in craftsmanship as [Gregor] has... he writes now with a clarity and transparency which leaves no place for either self-deception or self-conscious artifice."
— Robert Carter, *Modern Poetry Studies*

"The poems are so rich in descriptive experiences that are common to man universally that they give the reader a sense of relationship to the poet, which is pure art.... [The poems] are the kind of inner experiences that can supply a kind of strength and renewal because they shake the person awake to what he didn't remember he experienced.... A book to enjoy all your life."
—Virginia Brasier, *The Sun-Telegram*

"For twenty years I've been reading Arthur Gregor's poems with enthusiasm. What he has done is to give us, in textures and images consistently attractive, a spiritual vision of great originality. I should not care to live in a country where such poetry cannot be written. Gregor's volume of *Selected Poems* is a counter-witness, necessary and appropriate—a brilliant, beautiful book."
— Hayden Carruth

THE PAST NOW (1975)

"Gregor is famous for his expression of the tension in man created by the opposing lures of the postlapsarian world and the absolute world of Otherness.... For Gregor the essential man is not homo ludens but homo desiderans, man the desirer; this book is a gripping, dramatic record of a man living between the two outposts of hope and despair.... These poems can be read singly but they gain considerably from each other, like chapters of a narrative.... Highly recommended. A book of purity, integrity and distinction."
— Philip Dacey, *Prairie Schooner*

"'Spiritual' is a word so bedraggled by abuse as to be suspect; but to apply it to Gregor's poetry is to restore its strictest usage.... In Gregor's work, the past is never the past; it is alive in every aspect of the poem. The danger for poetry which has a strong spiritual force at its center is that the poems may become remote from the immediate and tangible. Gregor's most impressive accomplishment is his ability to make the spiritual intensely apprehended by the senses... the reader has a clear sense of the poet's intention of engaging major issues.... To take on this scale of intention is to work in high altitude without a net."
— Josephine Jacobsen, *The Nation*

"For thirty years Arthur Gregor has been writing poems that have moved ever more firmly and beautifully toward the expression of spiritual awareness. Yet he has never relied on conventional religious terms. Gregor himself is creating an archetype, a primal image. His poetry is strictly his own, the lucidity a real triumph...the best of their kind that we have had in many years.... Almost all of the poems are fine, and the book as a whole a warm and deeply moving statement."
— Hayden Carruth, *Harper's*

"When the sweetness of an Arthur Gregor poem is combined with the hard light of intellect (dark as such light often must be), the result is superb and gratifying art.... Gregor is a poet of 'glittering place,' one of those contemporary cartographers who hopes to redraw the old confluences of soul and body. His simplicity and clarity of language and his accuracy of memory are the proper tools for his Platonic enterprise."
— *Ohio Review*

EMBODIMENT (1982) (The Sheep Meadow Press)

"An enterprise that is frankly Rilkean in its 'struggle toward absolute verities' and its emphasis on praise as the poet's proper activity.... The book reveals a remarkable steadfastness of purpose. Several critics have applauded Mr. Gregor for the dignity and spirituality of his verse, and these qualities are in ample evidence throughout the volume."
— *The New York Times Book Review*

"Beautiful passages of descriptive poetry run like rich veins through the interior of (his) book. Gregor... is an explorer, a guide, a Rilkean singer peering into the paradoxical twists on the path to personal growth."
— Bill Tremblay, *American Book Review*

"Arthur Gregor is a passionate seeker after 'the pattern of being'.... The long, ambitious title poem is partly an effort to touch and to be touched by completeness.... Gregor often returns to the image of the face that lies behind all the faces he has met. The vision must be in the body if it is to be felt, but it must transcend the individual if it is to fulfill human longing. 'A Week in Venice' reaches a Zen-inspired climax. In addition to these provoking new poems, thirty-five selected poems from 1947 to 1974 give the reader valuable insights into the poet's growing self-awareness and increased power of language."
— James Finn Cotter, *The Hudson Review*

"The plight of human spirituality in this actual world, the special poignancy of our era of self-eroding values—these have been Arthur Gregor's concerns for years. Now, in his new poems, the greatness of his vision becomes fully evident, fully controlled: it is as if the sublime, as Longinus defined it, had somehow become alive again in our time. *Embodiment* is a very necessary book."
— Hayden Carruth

"I have read these pages several times and at each reading have discovered new depths
and beauties for my reward. How elusive these poems are, as the spirit turns in them,
and yet how replenishing, with their subtle, wavering music, their hints of elegy and
rapture! I believe Arthur Gregor is writing here at the peak of his power."
— Stanley Kunitz

"I find *Embodiment* impressive in Arthur Gregor's own characteristic style and pur-
suit. The quarry is the same, the means of capture ever more inventive and refined.
To have sustained such a long meditation, and have it grow in intensity, is a big
accomplishment."
— May Swenson

SECRET CITIZEN (1989) (Sheep Meadow)

"In this, his ninth book, Arthur Gregor continues his journey inward...he probes an
inner religious world in poetry that reaches eloquent heights of mystical experi-
ence.... The central eighteen-part work, ['The Poem of Heaven Within'] is firmly
grounded in both realms of spirit and matter, and springs from the poet's own brave,
tireless and fervent probing... a magnificent effort.... Echoes of Rilke's 'Duino Elegies'
and Eliot's 'Four Quartets' can be found and comparisons made, but on its own mer-
its this poem joins the august company of great meditative verse."
— James Finn Cotter, *The Hudson Review*

"I find the book's central poem 'The Poem of Heaven Within' a consummation of
all that Arthur Gregor has stood for. A rhapsody, a fervent meditation, all of it almost
delivered in one sustained breath, I am reminded of Stevens, especially moments in
'Sunday Morning,' Eliot in 'The Four Quartets,' and behind them the spiritual reach
of Dante. A poem so undeviating, so resolute, before its impulse and its purpose
would be extraordinary at any time, but it is especially remarkable now when the
daily and reductive hold sway. *Secret Citizen* is Arthur Gregor's most impressive work
to date."
— Theodore Weiss

THAT OTHER SIDE OF THINGS (2001) (Sheep Meadow)

"Ours is an age in which 'surfaces' of the world—even natural ones—seem hard,
shiny, impenetrable.... In *That Other Side of Things*, Arthur Gregor grapples with this
ubiquitous 'superficiality,' attempts to penetrate it, pass through, arriving 'beyond.' The
title of the collection, his eleventh, expresses this quest precisely. Reviving Rilke's
studied contemplation of 'things'.... Gregor has produced longish, gently-
rhymed...poems.... Gregor never lapses into the obscurities often bemuddling poet-
ry similarly motivated by philosophical yearning and speculation. A wistfulness does

294

emanate from several poems.... The laudable sincerity of this collection in fact lies...
in its conscious testing of the validity of a particularly deep and moving form of
wishful thinking."
— John Taylor, *POETRY*

"...[T]his reviewer finds it amazing how convincingly Gregor demonstrates that
beyond his words there are states of being, states of understanding, states of feeling,
none of which can be pinned down and yet... can be transmitted to us... this is what
happens in Gregor's poetry and continues in this collection.... I would assert that here
is an American poet who deserves a permanent place in the pantheon of world lit-
erature in English.... Arthur Gregor is certainly one of the last of the giants and must
be taken into account by any and every lover of poetry in English."
— Leslie Schenk, *World Literature Today*